Praise for Louise Rafkin's Rec

Different Daughters: A Book by Mo......

"Every Lesbian should have two copies of *Different Daughters,* one for herself and one for her mom . . ." —*Lambda Rising Book Report*

"A successful, human and dignified statement . . ."—Sarah Schulman, *The New York Native*

"The honest voices of these women are clear as they come to terms with their offsprings' lifestyles, providing a valuable perspective for others dealing with these complex issues."—*Library Journal*

"A compelling plea for reconciliation between parents and children."—*Booklist*

"*Different Daughters* is a lot like our mothers themselves, at their best: quietly powerful, deeply affecting, and in the end, very beautiful."—*Equal Time*

"I hope lesbian daughters will courageously package this book off to their mothers."—*Belles Lettres*

Different Daughters "provides mothers with concrete evidence that others like them exist, face similar issues, and that accepting lesbianism is not only possible, but liberating. For that, lesbians and their mothers can be grateful."—*Plexus*

"A great Valentine's or Mother's Day gift, but read it yourself before you send it."—*Newsmagazine for Alberta Women*

"I would urge you to buy this book and read it yourself and then pass it on to your mother . . ."—*Bay Area Reporter*

"Books are meant to be treasures and this one is."—*Bay Windows*

"Unique and heart-warming . . ."—*Chicago Outlines*

Unholy Alliances: New Women's Fiction

". . . A beautiful, well-crafted collection that offers us not only an unsparing recognition of the world's faults and our own, but also the hope of transcending them."—*Gay Community News*

". . . Masterful renderings that will stay with the reader for a long long time."—Margaret Randall, *Guardian*

"Reads like a sacrilegious hymn that manages some almost startling harmonies."—*Lambda Rising Book Report*

Different Mothers

Sons and Daughters of Lesbians Talk About Their Lives

Edited by Louise Rafkin

Cleis Press

Pittsburgh • San Francisco

Published in the United States by Cleis Press Inc., P.O. Box 8933, Pittsburgh, Pennsylvania 15221, and P.O. Box 14684, San Francisco, California 94114.

Printed in the United States.
Cover illustration: Pacha Wasiolek
Cover design: Cecilia Brunazzi/Louise Rafkin
Typesetting: CaliCo Graphics
Logo art: Juana Alicia

First Edition.
10 9 8 7 6 5 4 3 2 1

Library of Congress Cataloging-in-Publication Data

Different mothers : sons & daughters of lesbians talk about their lives / edited by Louise Rafkin. — 1st ed.
    p. cm.
    ISBN 0-939416-40-9 (cloth) : $24.95. — ISBN 0-939416-41-7 (paper) : $9.95
    1. Children of gay parents—United States—Case studies.   2. Lesbian mothers —United States—Case studies.   I. Rafkin, Louise, 1958-
HQ777.8.D54   1990
306.874—dc20
                                                            90-2529
                                                             CIP

Different Mothers

Grateful Appreciation . . .

To the women who helped me interview, without whose help the geographical diversity in the book could never have been realized: Stacy Jolles, Elana Dykewomon, Susan Jill Kahn, Lesléa Newman, Carol Genee, and Zelda Demmel. Also to Bárbara Selfridge, Ana MacFarlane, Melanie Braverman, Sarah Grey Thompson, and the biweekly P-town writer gals for editing help.

To Pendekkar for guidance in the art.

To the Fine Arts Work Center for space, heat and time. To Sparky, my beloved companion. To A.S.J. for loving support.

To the parents of the kids in this book who braved hearing the good, the bad and the—sometimes—ugly. Ultimately, there is beauty here. We tumble, stumble and stride forward, with hope.

This book is for Serena, Carolina, and Koko.

Contents

Introduction

Louise Rafkin

There's no doubt about it, America has gone baby crazy. And lesbians are certainly not exempt: we're smack in the middle of our own "gayby" boom.

There have always been and always will be women who come out as lesbians after marriage and divorce, and the children of these heterosexual unions have forever been a part of our communities. But now with old-fashioned and not-so-old-fashioned methods of conception more available, and adoption and foster parenting increasingly more accessible to both gays and lesbians, we're joining the ranks of proud parents by the thousands.

I have no doubt that lesbians of parenting age face issues similar to those of our straight counterparts. Over the past few years I have considered parenthood several times, and the questions I mulled over seemed basically the same as those considered by my heterosexual friends. Could I handle the commitment, the time restraint and the financial and emotional burden of being a parent? What about my relationships, both with friends and lovers? What is the feasibility of single parenthood? How do I feel about having an only child?

But in addition to these across-the-board considerations, I also had to tackle issues foreign to "thirtysomething" heterosexuals: What about co-parenting possibilities? What about conceiving with an unknown donor? A known donor? A friend? What kinds of problems would my child have being the daughter or son of an "out" lesbian and growing up in an alternative family?

It would be wonderful to think that being a lesbian is a private issue, one that doesn't include or affect those around us. But unfortunately lesbianism is not just a matter of who we bring into our bedrooms. In a society that still fears and condemns homosexuals, being lesbian deeply affects our parents and our families. Parents of perfectly content lesbians often feel guilt, anger, shame, or feelings of failure, and parents of not-so-happy lesbians often blame lesbianism for "ruining" their children's lives. Yet all of our lives are far more complicated than can be explained by these simple theories. And, of course, many of these feelings change over time when understanding and communication are nurtured to engender respect and appreciation. But what remains true is that our families—mothers, fathers, brothers, sisters and children—do have feelings about our sexual preference. Their lives, both their emotional lives and public lives, are affected by our lifestyles.

Children of lesbians live with the acute awareness of having lesbian mothers, although their feelings often take a different tack than those of parents of lesbians. Parents, as adults, can choose to withdraw from their children's lives if they can't handle things, and in many drastic cases they do. Children of lesbians cannot often leave their mothers, and usually they don't want to. The parent/child relationship is more dependent and therefore somewhat more complicated than those between adults and their grown lesbian offspring.

I learned from putting together my first book, *Different Daughters: A Book by Mothers of Lesbians*, that through listening to the stories and concerns of those we love we can better understand each other and improve our relationships. In interviewing the thirtysomething(!)

children and young adults in this book, I have attempted to give voice to the concerns of those people who are most affected by our parenting choices: children who are growing up with or have grown up with lesbian mothers. In our society we don't often listen to children. And in this instance, these are the very people who have the most to say, and need most to be heard.

This book includes the stories of children of lesbians from heterosexual unions, and those from both foster and adoptive families. There are children with one mother, two mothers or those with a host of co-mothers and stepparents. There are children who have fathers, no father, "donor-daddies," and gay fathers. There are children who have grown up in the heady seventies on lesbian land in the midst of lesbian separatism, and those who are being raised in quiet, closeted families in the Midwestern Bible Belt. The contributors range in age from five and a half to forty and span many different religions, cultures and sexual preferences.

Many of the voices in this book assure us that lesbians are making fine parents and creating wonderful families. So often an interview would end with a vehement statement along the lines of, "My mom's the best mom in the world, whatever she is!" From these stories we gather strength and encouragement. Parenting is a gamble and a risk, and lesbianism is an added unknown variable. But regardless of society's pressures and stigmas, it seems that many kids see past the difficulties and see possibilities that even their heterosexually raised counterparts are blind to.

But some of these stories are difficult to read. A few have pain written into every word. There is talk of divorce, of sexual abuse, of what we would now call "bad parenting." But in every story—both the positive and the not so positive—there are issues raised that have to do with lesbianism, and ones that simply point to problems in parenting. All who have done time in therapy know that childhood can be hell even under the most benign of circumstances. So many of the stories are fraught with problems common to *all* children and it's terribly important to remember this.

Sometimes it's easy to unravel whether a complaint about a mother has to do with her lesbianism. Sometimes this is not so easy to sort through. When a sixteen-year-old complains about not being able to stay out after midnight, is that an issue related to the mother's lesbianism? No, but if the sixteen-year-old is clever, he may try to pin it on that. In other cases it's more difficult to figure. There are kids in this book who have great problems with their mother's choice of partners, or changing of partners. Are these problems common to all children of single parents who may find themselves thrown together with "boyfriends" or even stepparents, or does lesbianism make a difference here? It's hard to know. Like parents of lesbians who say they don't mind their daughter's sexual preference, but they *hate* her short haircut, figuring out what's what can get complicated. (Is the haircut a result of her lesbianism or just a preference for easy hair care?) One boy, the child of two now split-up co-mothers, who travels with his brother between two households, summed up his main problem at the close of his interview: "The hardest thing about my life right now is that both my moms are vegetarians."

So there!

However, there are issues that emerge through these narratives that are clear and resounding and definitely have to do with lesbianism. Like peer pressure. It seems as though the issue of lesbianism first makes some sort of concrete difference to our children's lives around the first grade. It's hard for kids to be different, and having a lesbian mother is a real difference regardless of whether that is compounded by not having a father, or having a co-mother with a mohawk. When they start to feel different from other kids, there are usually feelings, some of which are painful and not easy to deal with.

Almost every contributor talks about keeping mom's lesbianism a secret, from school friends, from neighbors, and sometimes from other family members. There are ways kids get around talking about their families, by ignoring the probings of curious classmates, explaining away girlfriends and co-mothers as "aunts" or "roommates," or through blatant lying. It was difficult to discover just how much children carry the burden of social stigma. But I was also overwhelmed by the bravery of some of these kids, many of whom had never talked to anyone about their mother's lesbianism until being interviewed for this book. Some of these kids had been carrying their secrets five and ten years! But regardless of their courage, it's difficult to see children taking such responsibility for such heavy stuff, even though I realize that kids often carry secrets, some of which, like sexual abuse and alcoholism, are a lot more toxic than a parent's homosexuality.

And many of the kids who are keeping secrets are doing so for serious reasons. In several situations custody battles were major threats to the children's stability. For lesbian mothers being in the closet often means having your children in there with you. A situation in one Kansas household nearly broke my heart. The ex-husband has threatened a messy custody battle if his kids ever say *anything* about their mother's lesbianism. Meanwhile, every third weekend he has them to his house, where he and his current wife feed them anti-lesbian bigotry and other prejudiced tidbits. And, yes, the court backs this horrific situation.

In another story, "Of Lesbian Descent," a now-grown Kyneret Hope describes the custody battle that she and her mother waged when she was eleven. She then details her escape from her father's oppressive household, traveling alone underground back to her mother's home several states away. We'd like to think things are changing—and they are—only not fast enough.

All but a few of the children in the book keep their mother's sexual preference from someone, for all or part of their lives, even if they live in places like San Francisco. What does it mean for our children to hide their experiences? What will it mean in the long run? What are the by-products of this shame? Thankfully, it seems that after the precarious peer pressure years, junior high and high school, things ease off and there is more openness and acceptance on both sides of the parenting puzzle. There are several stories here from older "children" who attest to having come out of difficult childhoods full of appreciation and gratitude for their mothers and the openness and opportunity for growth that having a lesbian mother has provided them. As one man, now through his growing-up difficulties and well into his twenties, states, "If lesbianism is not made a problem it won't show up as one."

All this sounds heavy, and parenting surely is. But there are many helpful hints here for mothers who want to ease their kids through some of the hard times. One Florida teen, whose life became pretty miserable when her mother's lover came out on the Oprah Winfrey show, asserts that mothers should respect their kids' wishes when it comes to being out. She reckons that lesbian bumper stickers on visiting cars and lesbian books in the living room should be negotiated so that everyone in the household feels comfortable. Many kids said it was difficult to bring friends home because of lesbian books and other "paraphernalia."

Other suggestions for parenting pop up here and there. Most kids felt it was in their best interest to know as soon as possible about their mother's sexuality, so there are no surprises later on which might bring on feelings of betrayal. Those who were surprised, like Carla Tomaso, who writes of several traumatic times when she walked in on her mother in intimate relations with women, felt angry and confused. Other kids felt like new lovers in their mother's lives are especially hard if one is not used to sharing mom with anyone else. And relationship breakups are crises that are difficult for everyone to handle. Though several lesbian custody cases are now in the courts, it seems like even in those with smooth custody agreements, the lack of stable long-term relationships is difficult for any kid.

Sexuality is an issue that seems to be given more airplay in lesbian families. Most of the kids in the book who are past puberty feel that their options and understanding of their own sexuality have been greatly helped by open communication with their mothers and/or mothers' friends. Several have tried bisexuality; some are homosexual themselves. But a few contributors mentioned that their own sexuality was especially scrutinized by their mothers, as well as by the lesbian community. To some this felt like an invasion of privacy. But overall, most kids felt their mothers would accept them whatever their sexual preference.

Fathers, or lack of fathers, is also an issue which reoccurs. For those without fathers, not knowing the identity of their fathers was usually a deep worry. One ten-year-old tells of watching men on the street who fit the donor description of her father, trying to figure out who could "be the one." For several children, not knowing their father was not a problem at all. For one ten-year-old girl, finding out her donor was a friend of the family was shocking, and though it felt to her like the "missing puzzle piece" of her life, it remains a piece with rough edges. Two young girls adopted from India allude to the mystery not only of their parents, but of their culture as well.

But for some of the younger interviewees, having two mothers seemed a lot more advantageous than having a mother and a father. A few said that they had heard bad things about fathers, that fathers are people who are "mean and spank you." One six-year-old said that the reason she didn't tell her friends about having two mothers was that they'd be jealous! Another noted that "daddies are dumb as bubble gum."

Those curious about the effect of bringing up boys without fathers will find that the boys in this book seem as well-adjusted as any, if not more so. In some cases boys were more adversely affected by lesbians who have problems and attitudes about boy children than by not having fathers. In fact, though we might hope the negative attitudes some lesbians have about men shouldn't carry over to boys and young men, it seems this isn't quite the case. I'm hoping those who still feel negative towards boy-children will read the advice of twenty-eight-year-old Michael in "A Lousy Deal" who tells of the negative effects of such prejudice and hatred.

For some this will be a negative read. It's not always smooth sailing for parents of any persuasion, and those lesbians who think they can do things differently, and assuredly better, than our straight counterparts might find this book a bit of a setback. We're great people, but we're not always great parents, and the world's not such a great place—yet. But for me there's optimism here. Almost every story ends with an incredible affirmation of love and respect by the child for his or her mother or mothers. It seems that lesbians are bringing up kids who are more socially responsible, less prejudiced, more open to difference. Many of these kids have an insight into their feelings and emotional life that I would have never dreamed of at their age. Most of these kids will grow up straight, but with an awareness of possibility that I certainly didn't have. As one seven-year-old put it, "I maybe want to be a dentist, but I don't know if I want to be a lesbian."

I am writing this introduction to parents, but in my heart I have put together this book for kids. It's a pretty heavy thing, being a kid in our society. And as many of us who are now unraveling our Wonder Bread years know, it's something that—sometimes unfortunately— stays with us forever. I'm hoping that this book will find its way into the hands and hearts of children of many ages, those who feel isolated and alone and who need to know there are other children out there who have lived with the same problems they are facing. I'm also hoping that mothers (and "aunties" and godmothers and siblings) will read these stories to younger children so they can hear about other kids such as themselves. With luck, *Different Mothers* will be made available in schools, for both counselors and libraries. Nearly every inter- viewee was curious about the other kids I was talking to. What were they like, where were they? Perhaps this book can be a kind of community for those kids of lesbians who feel all alone out there.

But of course, this book is also for lesbians considering parenthood. Read it and weep, read it and laugh. (Read it and prepare for those teen years! Yikes!) There are those here who have faced the same problems, silences, and situations that you will. And there are amazing people represented here, lives full of hope and struggle and progress.

I myself have backed away from parenting, for the time being. But who knows? There are kids in here I'd love to call my own. We're all learning from each other, and I'm convinced we're on the right track.

Louise Rafkin
June 1990

Just Different, That's All

Serena

I'm seven and a half and I live in Albany, California. I'm about to go into second grade. I live with my mother now, but other times I've lived with lots of women. My mom's a nurse. I take kung-fu and want to be a therapist when I get older. I enjoy telling stories.

I started knowing my mother was different when I was five and I started school. A lot of people there were straight, and my mother started to talk to me about how she was different. But it wasn't until I started first grade that I really realized things. Nothing was really different, but my mom started to ask me what I felt about her being a lesbian mother, because a lot of people weren't lesbian mothers. I asked my mom what a lesbian was, and she said it was like, instead of a man and woman being together, it was two women that were in love. Then I knew what a lesbian was.

I knew it was different to be a lesbian, but it's really

hard to think about. I brought this book to first grade for my sharing day. It's called *Many Mommies*. My teacher had this whole big talk about it. She talked about all different kinds of families. Then she read the book to everyone and told me it was a really great book. A couple kids said it was a good book, but no one said anything else.

Now I know a few other kids who have lesbian moms, and this makes me feel better. I know a lot of lesbian women, but not a lot of lesbian moms. Lesbian moms seem different than married women. It seems like married women get a lot more help; they don't have to work so much. Their husbands go to work and so they get to stay home with the kids. When I go to kids' houses who have a mom and a dad, it seems like they're really rich, like they have a lot of money.

Maybe it seems easier to be married, but then that might be hard because maybe straight women get in fights with their husbands a lot. My mom works all the time, and I wonder if maybe she had a husband she could stay home with me in the summer and I wouldn't have to go away to my grandparents'.

When I go to my grandparents' for the summer I get spoiled. We have ice cream all the time. But it's hard because we can't really . . . you see, my grandma and grandpa are kind of mad that my mom is not with a man and that everybody else is married. They don't even like saying the word lesbian. They don't talk about it, but my mom talks about it and she told me they didn't like it. I don't like the way they feel about her.

They feel that women should be with men. So do most of my aunts and uncles. They don't tell me this stuff, but grownups keep quiet about things like that. That don't think children should hear that kind of stuff, or maybe they don't think kids should know about different types of families. Maybe they think their family is the way all families are supposed to be. Or maybe they're embarrassed. Maybe I should send this book to the whole family!

But you know, when I was visiting my uncle, he would sit there at the dinner table and talk about business. Business, business, business. I got kind of bored talking about business at dinner. When I go out with my mom for dinner we talk about kung-fu, or sometimes we talk about my mom being a lesbian mother. It's more interesting.

I like having lots of friends who are lesbians; they take care of me and take me places. When I lived with a bunch of lesbian women, I liked coming home because there was always someone there. I have a couple of men friends who are really nice guys. Sometimes I feel like I kind of miss out on some stuff, but I like having a lesbian mother. Sometimes I like being different. Sometimes I feel special being different. Other times I wish my mom was married and that I had a dad. It depends.

It seems like everyone who has a dad also has a brother or a sister. It seems like lesbian mothers usually have one kid. But maybe it's better they only have one kid; it's less to handle. Sometimes when I want somebody to play with, I wish I had a brother or sister. Other times I'm glad I'm an only kid. There's nobody to step on my sandcastles when I make them! Maybe if I had a brother we'd fight a lot. My mom is happy she didn't have seven kids like her mom did.

I don't tell other kids about my mom. At school it kind of bothers me because when we play or tell stories, there's always a mom and a dad. There's never a mom and a mom or a dad and a dad—always just a mom and a dad. Some kids ask me who is my dad, and why I don't live with him. I don't really know how to explain it to them. I say I don't really have a dad, but then they say that's impossible. So see, it's like they don't believe me or I have to pretend I have a dad because I feel like I have to have one.

What really bothers me is when my friends come over and then they get into this whole divorce thing. They ask if my parents are divorced or what. I say yes, but then they ask me if I know my dad. So I tell them no, not really. Then they ask who he is, and what does he do, and I hate that. I really don't like it. But then they only talk about it for a couple seconds and then they want to play something. They don't want to talk about dad stuff for very long.

Sometimes I ask my mom about my dad but . . . you see, I wonder about him. I don't know where he is. I don't think my mom knows either. It's just hard to know that other kids have dads. Everybody else has a dad.

My mom has had a couple relationships with other women, but I didn't realize it at the very time. I just thought that we were sleeping over at their house, or they were sleeping over. It's really okay with me, but sometimes I like just being with her and nobody else. I like spending alone time with my mom. I like living with just my mom, but I wish it was in a house, not an apartment. In this apartment I have to be really quiet, and I don't enjoy being quiet.

When I grow up I want to live with someone; I don't know if I want to get married and I don't know if I want to have kids. It seems like you need a lot of money to have kids. Sometimes I feel strange having a lesbian mom; sometimes it's hard, and sometimes it's just different. It's good to have all kinds of families. My mom is the best mom in the world and I want that to be in this book.

Back and Forth

James

I'm sixteen, mostly Chinese, but one-quarter Irish. I live in Chicago, half the time with my father and the other half with my mother. I like riding and fixing bikes.

I was about four and my father was working overseas when my mother and he divorced. She had changed from being a straight to being a lesbian.

When I was two and a half years old, my mother started seeing her first woman lover. I could tell they were together. All throughout my childhood I was around adults, so I really understood my surroundings. I had intelligent conversations with my parents' friends and was into acting sort of adult. Her lover came to live with us and stayed until I was ten. She had a son seven years older than I, so he came and lived with us too. I loved this because her son and I had been best friends since I was born. My father was living in Singapore after they separated, and he wrote, but I didn't know him that well. During this part of my childhood it didn't seem that different to me to have a lesbian mom. My mother's lover was like my co-mother.

When my mother and her lover split up, things got a bit messy. Before they split up they were having fights, and about this time my father came back from overseas. My mother had a nervous breakdown and my father wasn't very good with children, so I got carted off to my aunt's house to live. The result was that I wasn't very happy at my aunt's house, with my cousins, and I wasn't being treated well there. But I lived there three and a half years. I didn't see my mother for about a year of this time because she was recuperating. After a year or so I saw her every two weeks and went back and forth to my aunt's. When I finally told my dad about how I didn't like living at my aunt's, I ended up at his house and then went back and forth to my mother's. It's been like this for the last three years. It's fun because if I get sick of one parent I can always go to the other.

I talk to my mother's ex-lover every now and then. My mother recently split up with her second girlfriend. These breakups don't bother me that much, because I still get to see the people that she has broken up with.

I don't talk to anyone at school about my mom. I know other sons and daughters of lesbians, and sometimes I talk to them. There is some cover-up that kids of lesbians have to do, because otherwise you are accused of being gay yourself. If I came out and said my mother was gay, I'd be treated like an alien. Sometimes I hear prejudice stuff against gays, but I can't point it out, because otherwise it would look suspicious. I don't laugh at anti-gay jokes, but I don't outrage against them either.

My grandparents—both sets—are pretty old and basically stay out of my mother's life. Her parents especially really got upset when she came out. They thought that my parents would get married and stay together forever and ever. I think part of it is being Chinese and Christian. Both those things made it pretty hard for them to accept.

News about my mother leaked into the Chinese church that they went to, and they were pretty mad. They said my mother had disgraced their family name. At that time they used to take me to church with them to prove to everyone that I was okay and not gay. When my mom first came out to them, they totally ignored her and told her they didn't consider her their daughter. And when I was younger they tried to talk to me about my mother, and they tried to influence me to tell my mother to go straight again, and to get back with my father. Now they are more understanding and have finally accepted that she is gay and is not going to go back to my father.

I've talked to my mom about how she came out. We talk about lots of things. I can talk to my mother about girls because she likes the same sex I do! What an advantage. I'll show her pictures of girls I like and she'll say, "Oh, yes, she looks interesting." It's nice to get her opinion. It goes two ways; I talk to her about her life, too.

I used to go to the lesbian coffeehouse. I used to hang out there and meet my mom's friends, but now I'm too old and I can't go there any more. I think boys can't go there after they are about eleven or twelve. This makes me feel restricted, but I understand why they want lesbian-only space away from men. But at the same time I felt sad about it, and I think the women I knew there felt sad that I'm now too old to go there. I respect their rules and decisions, but I didn't like being excluded. But the rule against boys was made in 1974—the year I was born—and it doesn't seem like they're going to change it just for me.

I have an open mind because of my mom; my mind is not what I'd call "straight." I keep open about what might happen in the future. I don't turn away people at school who I know are gay. But it's hard, because after a point if you support them, they think you are gay. I try to go up to that point. Since AIDS has come up, the gay boys at school are very discriminated against. They are automatically accused of having AIDS. In school I've said a couple words, mostly in seminars and discussions, that I hope have triggered other people's thoughts, so that they might change their thinking.

My mom and I have a great relationship. Stuff comes up between us—like it does for everyone—but we talk about everything.

The Telling

Lisa Perry

I am twenty-one years old and live in Indiana. I'm in my junior year of college where I'm majoring in psychology. I'm also a cat lover and photography buff.

I can still remember vividly the night my mother told me she was gay. Every night she and I got ready for bed at the same time. She would usually be soaking in the tub when I went into the bathroom to brush my teeth. This was the time when we filled each other in on our days and talked about things. For about six months she hadn't been home much, and we hadn't been communicating very well. I was seventeen and felt neglected, because when she did grace the family with her presence it was either for a very brief time or it was with a friend. She and I had stopped having wonderful mother-daughter chats or going to brunch like we used to, and like I thought we still should. Sometimes when we did make plans they would fall through, or she would bring a friend along.

I gradually became frustrated, angry and hurt. It felt

as though my mother wanted nothing to do with me. The hate and pain grew so great inside of me that when she was around I did everything in my power to be a bitch. After a while I got tired of feeling so full of hate, and so I sought out some answers from one of her friends. She was sympathetic to my feelings, and told me that my mother was wondering if she still wanted to be married. She told me that my mother was having some feelings that she didn't know how to deal with. This confused me even more.

I started to think that my mother was a very self-centered person who didn't give a damn about her family. Then, that night in the bathroom, all my questions were answered.

I'm fuzzy about how the conversation got started, but I remember my mother trying to tell me she was a lesbian. I was standing in front of the mirror, picking at my face, and she was in the bathtub, telling me about how she felt about her friend Lori. By the time she had finished she was on the verge of tears, and I realized that it was probably one of the hardest things she had ever had to do.

I asked her if she was going to get divorced, and she told me that more than likely she would. Then I kissed her goodnight and went to bed. I didn't cry, or scream. I just slept. It felt like all of us were getting divorced; the separation and loss would hurt all of us. I think now that the reason I didn't get emotional was because I finally had some answers to my questions. The reason I had been "neglected" was because she hadn't known who she was, much less how to relate to us in a time when it took all of her energy to carry herself through the most exhausting event in her life. And for that, I forgive her.

Unfortunately, telling me about what was going on

was not the worst of what was to come. We had to tell my sixteen-year-old brother. My parents wanted to do this with a family counselor, and I did not want to be there. I don't like confrontations, and I knew this was going to be a big one. I had to go anyway. David, my brother, was shocked. He hadn't seen the signs and didn't know there was anything wrong. Everyone was crying except me. I hated being there. The counselor asked me what I felt, and I felt like saying I wanted to walk out of the room and never come back. But I didn't. I mumbled something and stared at the wallpaper. At the end of the session he said he thought we were all going to be fine, but that he was worried about me because I wasn't showing any emotion. I told him not to worry.

Before all the dust settled, I went to see my mother's therapist because she was worried that I was not showing any grief. Inside I had decided that I was going to do everything possible to get my family through all of it. I thought of myself as the "helper"—I did whatever anyone wanted me to do. I supported everyone, which is how I got my mind off the divorce. I helped my mother shop for a house, and I helped her move. I was there if anyone needed me. I was there for my grandparents to talk to because they thought my parents' marriage was perfect—as if I had all the answers! I listened to my father when he was lonely and needed to talk. Needless to say, I was a good pair of ears. I took everything in, accepted everything. I have since been told this was pretty strange behavior. But what else could I do? I could have been in denial or rebellion like my brother, but that seemed to me like wasted energy.

I know my mom went through a time of feeling very guilty, and I think she still feels this sometimes. I look at what happened as something she could not have helped. It was not her choice to be lesbian, any more that it is my choice to be heterosexual. I haven't decided whether homosexuality is genetic or environmental. Sometimes I am curious about it, and sometimes I just don't care.

At this point I can't imagine my parents being married, although they are still good friends. I can still feel my dad's pain, however, because he never wanted the divorce. Also, he got married six months after the divorce. That was hard!

Now when I think of my mom I think of Lori—her partner—and Lori's son, too. In the beginning I resented Lori some because she got more attention and time from my mother than I did. I felt like I should be my mother's first priority! But once I found out what was going on and saw how they were together, I felt different. They have a partnership. They are best friends; they talk about everything—about things that make them mad, about how it feels to be women. And then they are lovers, too. They have the best of both worlds, the best of being lovers and being friends.

It's hard to find words for what Lori is to me. She is an amazing person, my mother's companion, partner, lover and friend. To me she is a sister, mother, a guiding light and someone I can go to whenever I need to. She has become a very important part of my life.

Her son Joey is a miracle. He is a red-headed ten-year-old who has experienced more than any child his age should have. He learned about divorce and about his mother's sexual preference at such an early age. I'm not sure he completely understands it all. But he shows few scars and manages to be so enlightening and enthusiastic about his life. And sometimes, like any kid his age, he's still a pain in the ass!

I feel as though I've known Joey and Lori all of my life. They are my family. But now, two years after my parents split up, I am starting to feel the pain of that loss. When I recently came home from college, I missed not having one bed, one closet, or one house to settle into. I have to split up my vacations between the two houses, which doesn't make for very relaxing vacations. It's not just the inconvenience. The divorce happened my senior year in high school, and it felt like an end to my childhood and the beginning of my adult life. Like most people my age, sometimes I wish I could go back in time to when I was ten and things seemed easy. Now I can't even go back to the house I grew up in, because we sold it after the divorce.

But there is no going back, only ahead. It comes down to the fact that from 1976 to 1987 my mother was a very unhappy person. I'm still not sure how she kept her sanity all those years. It took all of her to do what she did. I have decided that no matter who she is, I am going to love her and support her forever.

Throughout this whole ordeal I felt as though we have become closer than ever before. Once I knew about what was happening with my mother, it was much easier to communicate. The secrets were no longer necessary. We don't know everything about each other—which is good—but sharing makes us closer.

I still wonder why my mother took so long to tell me what was going on. I have a feeling that if I asked about this, she would say that she told me as soon as she fully knew herself.

The Missing Piece

Annie

I'm ten and I live with my two moms in San Francisco. Diane is a nurse and she lives upstairs with her girlfriend. Linda lives downstairs and she works at a downtown job. I live both upstairs and downstairs. I didn't know my dad until we found him last year. His name is Tom and he lives with his lover Tim nearby.

Now that I've found my dad, Tom, I don't think there's much difference having lesbian moms. But before I found Tom, I thought a lot about who my dad was. It felt great to find him because I hadn't known him for ten years, my whole life. It was weird, because before I found out he was my dad I knew Tom as a friend. Diane and Linda didn't know he was my dad either. He had given his sperm to a friend, who gave it to another friend, and then she gave it to us. One of those people was in Holland, and when she came back we called her up and she found the other friend, and then that friend contacted Tom. So when they told me "We found your dad!" I was jumping up and down for joy. And then when they said he was Tom, I sat down in my chair, because I already knew him, and I had never suspected he was my dad.

I wanted to find my dad because it was hard knowing I had a dad but not knowing who he was. It was like there was a missing piece. I didn't know if he was dead. I didn't know if he was alive. The information we had about him said he was living in San Francisco, but he could have moved. I didn't know what had happened to him. I just knew I wanted to find him so that missing piece would be filled. I don't really think it's important that everyone have a dad, but it was important to me because my moms told me that I had a dad. If they hadn't told me I had a dad, I probably wouldn't have thought anything of it. But because they told me, it meant I had to find him.

Before he gave his sperm, Tom filled out an application form, and my moms had this form. When I was growing up I always wanted to talk about what was on it. There was stuff about what he looked like, and what he did for a living. I used to ask questions about him all the time. My moms would tell me what was on the form, like "He's short, he has brown hair and brown eyes. He has a mustache." I wanted to know things about his background, like who he was and where he came from. We knew he was Italian. But I wanted to know all this other stuff. On the street I used to look for people that sounded like that description of him.

It's only been a few months since I found him, and it still feels a little weird. It feels funny because I never would have suspected that my dad was Tom. I get together with him sometimes. We hang out together. The first night I met him as my dad, we got to know each other. He came over for dinner with his lover. After that night it was like we had known each other for a real long time. He's funny and he makes a lot of jokes because he's a comedian. Now it's like I have two dads because of Tim, Tom's lover. Things seem different in my life now that I have a dad, but I don't really know why.

I only told my two best friends about all this; it was okay because I know them so well. My best friend talked to me when her parents got divorced, so it was easy to talk with her about my life. We've been in the same class together since kindergarten. Other people at school know that I have two moms, but that's all they know. I don't tell people because there's only a couple kids in the whole school who have lesbian moms. Next year I'm going to a school where there are lots of kids with lesbian moms, and even some of the teachers are lesbian and gay. I think things will be easier there.

I've been with kids who have said awful things about lesbians and gays, and this made me feel rotten inside. I ignore this stuff. I don't like to say anything, because sometimes these kids are my friends, and I don't want to get in fights with them.

When I talk about my moms I call them "my two moms." I don't talk about the fact that they used to be lovers. Some kids think it's neat that I have two moms, because if I ask one for something and she says no, I can ask the other one and she could say yes! Sometimes it's hard to have two mothers, but I think that is hard whether or not the moms are lesbians. Like what if I won an airplane ticket and I could only take two people? It would be hard to figure out who to take. But I think you get more love with two moms. I know other kids have a mom and a dad, but I think that moms give more love than dads. This may not be true, but it's what I think.

Before I was born, Linda and Diane lived together, but after they broke up they decided they both needed their own space. I think they broke up before Diane was pregnant, or maybe it was during the time she was pregnant. Diane has a girlfriend now, and Linda said she might want to have a girlfriend soon. I'm used to Diane's girlfriend because I have known her all my life, ever since I was born. But I don't like it when Linda talks about getting a girlfriend. It seems weird that she might have one. I'm so used to it being just her and me. I like it this way. If Linda got a girlfriend, it would take a long time for me to adjust.

I have a sister who lives in New York. Linda had her a long time ago and she gave her up for adoption. But we found her when she was twenty-one. She's getting married in May. I've only seen her once, but I talk on the phone to her.

I always knew my moms were lesbians, but I never really asked anything about it. I only asked about my dad. When I was young, Diane used to go to demonstrations, and she used to sing these songs about lesbian and gay people. I went with her to demonstrations, and I guess I figured things out because of those songs. I sang the songs, too.

I think my life is the same as it would be if I had straight parents. My moms let me see things any way I want to. If I want to be straight, that's okay with them. They don't force me to go any which way. They say it's okay to be whatever you are, that it's okay to be your own person.

I don't like homophobia. There's no reason for people to be scared of gays and lesbians. They are just human beings like everyone else. In the future I think there might be less homophobia, so things might be better. But I don't really know if things really will be different. When I get older I might feel more comfortable telling people. Right now I don't really know what would make things easier. Sometimes talking about things helps. Sometimes keeping your mouth shut helps, too.

When I grow up I want to be a writer. I want to write stuff like Roald Dahl writes. I write stories now and I put animals in my stories. Like I might take my turtle—his name is Speedy Gonzales—and say that he has *Playboy* magazines under his shell and write a story about that. My favorite things are reading and playing basketball. I play soccer on a team. I like my life. The only thing I would change about my life is my neighborhood, because there's a lot of drugs around.

A Real Big Secret

Katie and Tessa O'Neal

Katie: I live in Kansas City. I like to read and do ballet, gymnastics, tap and jazz. My favorite group is New Kids on the Block. I'm in the fifth grade. I have a brother and a sister. We live with my mom and Rachel, who have been together five and a half years.

One day when I was about six, I woke up in the middle of the night from a bad dream, and I looked in the bedroom and saw Rachel and my mom sleeping together. The next day I was trying to hint at things because I knew something was up. So I asked them if they wore underwear to bed. They couldn't understand why I asked that. They said, "Why do you want to know?" They never told me either. They wouldn't say anything about it.

But I started to think they were more than friends. No one else I knew had a woman living with them. My mom told me to tell people that Rachel was our roommate. I was sort of scared. It felt funny. I didn't know if it was okay or not. And I didn't feel comfortable talking with them about it. I just found out they are gay, *officially*, two years ago. My mother told me out front when she started going to a gay church.

Before she told me, I used to tell my brother and sister that mom and Rachel were gay, and once my brother told my mom I said that. Then my mother read my diary, and I had written that she was gay. She was crying, and she asked me if I really wanted to know if she was gay. I told her no. I was too scared to know. I really didn't want to know. I didn't want to believe it. I kept thinking that it couldn't be. But underneath, I really knew.

I didn't understand how people didn't notice it! In their bedroom I'd see stuff lying around, like books about lesbians. But no one said anything. I have only told one friend. She is older than me, and she didn't say much except that she promised to keep it a secret. She is the only one I have told.

I never talk to my sister about it, because we don't feel comfortable talking about it. I guess I'm too chicken. I don't talk to my mother either. No one outside our family knows about my mom, just her friends. I consider this a *really* big secret. I don't feel like anyone is trustworthy. I don't think that if my best friend knew, she would ever come over to spend the night.

Rachel is like my second mom. I'd pick her over any other mom in the world, except my mom. When my mom and she had their first fight in front of us, we were so upset. We were all crying, and so were they. Mom took us to McDonald's and talked to us about it, and it was scary. Rachel left the house, and then she came back later and we were all so happy. Right then it seemed like we liked her better, but I think it's not really true. We like her and mom equal. They are our most favorite people in the whole entire world. But I'd hate to live in a fighting family. I think I like this way better than having a dad. I hear of so many kids who have dads and moms having screaming fights. Even though I was really little, I remember my dad hurting my mom. They were fighting, and he was strangling her against the wall. I was saying, "Let her go!" I remember some good times, too, but it seems to me the only times he was friendly to her was when he was around other people.

I thought of going to the school counselor to talk about things, but I worried about him telling my teachers. I think if the teachers knew about my mom, they would treat me different. I think they would gossip about me. I wouldn't like that. Maybe I'd like to talk to someone not connected to my school, but it doesn't really hurt me not talking to anyone. I've done it for all these years.

Ever since second grade I have told people I live with Rachel and mommy. I said, "Rachel's our roommate and she lives downstairs." Now I say, "Rachel is a good friend of my mom's—they are *best* friends." There's this really prejudiced guy in my class; he hates blacks and everybody different. He's really into heavy metal. And because my best friend is black, he told me to hang out with my "own type." He always says stuff about men he thinks are gay; he calls them "gay-bobs." My dad is prejudiced like that, too.

My dad once saw this guy that was gay and he said, "Look!" and then he was really weird and said awful things about him. We go to gay church meetings. There are some really nice gay men there, and some kids who are really nice. They are friendlier than regular men. They come up and hug you and everything. But my dad hates gays.

He also hates Rachel living with us. Lots of times he

and his wife have told us that being gay is wrong. They say women should be with men, that or nothing. They also say whites should be with whites. It's really awful. And every three weeks we go there for the weekend. I hate it. And my stepmom treats us like trash. She hates us. We are like nothing in her life.

I've had lots of boyfriends. There is this really big geek in the fifth grade and everyone makes fun of him. But I kind of like him—and I'm really popular—and I think if people knew I liked him, they would hate me. Whenever I have the chance, I talk to him. I like all the geeks. But I wonder what will happen when I have boyfriends who find out about my mom. I wonder if they will still like me. And if I want to get married and the guy found out, would he still marry me? I guess if they can't take me how I am, they can't have me.

I think mothers should tell their kids right off if they are lesbians. If the kids think it's okay, great. If they think it's not okay, they'll get used to it. I thought it was very wrong the first time I heard about my mom. Maybe if people didn't like that their moms were gay, they could live with their fathers. But I wouldn't even think of that; I love living with my mom, whatever she is.

*Tessa: I'm thirteen and
in the seventh grade. I
love to ride horses and
have a horse named
Darling. My favorite
thing to do is read.
There's nothing I'd
rather do.*

When I was in second grade, I asked my mom if she was gay, and she said yes! We talked and she asked me what I thought being gay meant, and I said it's like you have two mothers or two fathers instead of a mother and father. From then on I didn't think there was anything wrong with it, because if this person I really admired was gay—my mother!—then it must be okay.

I never talk to anyone about it. Sometimes I talk to my mom about certain things. We have talked about how some gay women dress like men and how some men dress like women. I think that is really weird, and I don't understand why they do it. I think it must be really hard on their kids, too. What if they went and met their kids' teachers dressed like that? My mom and Rachel look like women, and they dress really normal. You wouldn't look at them on the street and know they were gay.

It's our private business and it's nobody else's, and so I don't tell anyone. If somebody found out, and they were really good friends, they probably wouldn't tell. If they did tell people and kids at school found out, I think I'd be a social reject. Kids think of AIDS or make fun of gay people, and they call them faggots. I don't really think it's these kids' fault, it's just the way they've been raised. I don't dislike them for thinking those things; they don't understand. All my friends love Rachel and my mom, and so they never think anything bad about them. People think that gay people are weird or different or strange, but gay people are just normal like everyone else.

I know that my father knows that my mother is gay. Once when we kids were in the the car and he was mad, he said, "When you get older I'm going to tell you something that will make you want to move in with me right away!" I thought, what does he think we are, stupid? He doesn't realize that we love our mother no matter what she is called or labeled. He is always putting gays down. Once he said, "They shouldn't let fags on TV." I think he is trying to make us think being gay is bad and turn us against our mother. But it's not working. I think he's immature. If he can't accept that other people are different from him, then he is really stupid. I'm thirteen and I can accept it—and I could accept it when I was six. And he is thirty-six and he can't accept it? Well, it makes me wonder about his brains.

I think it's good to let your children know you are homosexual, because if you are different, your children already know it at some level. If you keep it a secret, they might think that it is bad, because if you aren't talking about it, it must be something to hide.

I think it's good for kids with lesbian moms to talk with others who are the same age as they are. I used to go to a support group, and that was really good. There are always support groups for moms, but not always for kids. It's hard to talk to strangers about things that you don't want to get out. I think kids should talk to their parents and try to see things from their point of view. I've lived through this, and I know what it is like.

Editor's note: Katie and Tessa's dad has threatened their mother with a custody battle if anyone finds out she is in a lesbian relationship. This includes the children's teachers. In the county in which the parents divorced, no lesbians have ever won custody. In addition, because of state laws, the family cannot leave the state of Missouri until all their children are eighteen. "It's terrible that my kids have to live with this secrecy, but it's worth it because someday there will be time for openness," said Katie and Tessa's mother. "Life isn't easy out here in the Midwest. But we still manage to have a very happy family, and that's what's important. Our family is interesting and challenging, but certainly not more challenging than it is enjoyable."

Not
Us-and-Them

Kathleen C. Sloan   *I'm twenty-three, black, an only child and an aspiring photographer. I was raised in many places, but have lived in California since the late eighties.*

My parents divorced when I was three, so I've always known my mother as a lesbian. My mother has never hidden her lesbianism; she has always discussed everything with me since the time I was old enough to listen. I always knew what a lesbian was, and I always knew I had a choice as to what I would be. My mom and I are tight friends, good friends. Most people don't have this kind of friendship with their parents.

My mom has always been in the public eye. She's a political activist and has been active in civil rights and lesbian issues ever since I can remember. In the early seventies, she was one of the founding members of *Ms.* magazine with Gloria Steinem. I always thought her activism was fun. There were parades of people in the house, all active in different causes. She was away a lot when I was growing up, on speaking tours and working in the media, and I grew up a lot on my own. I've always been independent, and this really didn't bother me too much, because when we were together we were so close.

As a kid I went to the women's festivals and political marches. At one point we were close to Jessie Jackson. I've even given speeches myself. I remember one time when I was about six and my mother and Gloria Steinem were lecturing to the Mattel toy company. She mentioned me in her talk, and the audience wanted me to get up on stage. I got up there and started saying that I thought it was really bad that all the Tonka truck commercials had boys in them. I wanted to know how come Barbie and Easy-Bake ovens were only for girls. Even at that age, I had my own anti-sexist campaign going.

Everyone knows my mom. Women always come up to me and tell me how great she is, and how they heard her way back when, and how what she said changed their life. I'm known because of her. In one way this is great. There are a lot of women out there who could be there for me if I needed anything. But in some ways it's a slight hindrance, because now I am doing some recovery work and I go to anonymous meetings and I'm not really anonymous. I don't feel comfortable in meetings where everyone knows my mother. Being known in that way is difficult.

I never had problems because of my mom's lesbianism. When I was eight, my best friend was a girl called Marcie. We did everything together: played on the soccer team, the bowling team, stayed overnight at each other's houses nearly every night—everything. One night my mom had a party, and Marcie's mother suddenly stormed in and tore Marcie out of the house and told Marcie that she couldn't be friends with me. The next day Marcie came over and told me she couldn't see me anymore. She took all her things from my house, and her mother took her off the sports teams we were on together.

My mother suspects that Marcie's mother saw two women kissing on the porch. At the time she wrote Marcie's mother a letter explaining everything, about how she loved Marcie and had always been good to her and how her lesbianism didn't affect my life—or Marcie's. Her mother never responded, and that was the end of our friendship. That was also the first time that my mother's sexuality affected my life in any way, but although it upset me, I don't remember feeling as though it was my fault.

I figured if kids didn't like me because my mother was a lesbian, I didn't need them as friends. But once in junior high school my mother asked me to be on television with her, about something to do with gay rights, and I said no. They ended up showing a photo of me anyway. A girl from school, a real bully, saw the program and stood on the front steps of the school and started screaming that my mother was a faggot. All I could think of at the time was "She's not a faggot, she's a lesbian!" That's the only time I felt like I didn't want anyone to know about her, and I felt really uncomfortable for about a month. I just hated everyone hassling me.

Generally, lesbians with kids hang with other lesbians with kids. So growing up I had a support system of kids who were in the same situation that I was, and I didn't develop a complex. I think it's easier for me because my mother's never been in the closet, but she's been proud and open and out the whole of my childhood. I think that I've been able to feel comfortable because I don't have the feeling that she's ashamed or that there is anything to hide.

There were only a few times when my mother and I lived alone with each other. She always lived with her lovers, or we had housemates. Sometimes we lived in big communal houses. It was hard to get used to a new lover, especially if she decided she was going to be an authority figure in my life. This happens in straight relationships too, when parents get involved with new people. But when the lover relationship was over, these lovers would leave, saying they wanted to continue a relationship with me. But they never did. When the relationship was over, their relationships with me were also pretty much over.

My defense against this was that I never became attached to these women. Until very recently my mother never got involved with women who were mothers themselves, and so they weren't sensitive to my mom having a kid. I put up an emotional wall whenever my mom would say, "This is it; this is the relationship that's going to last forever." But I'd predict that it would end in such and such amount of time. I had slim expectations of her being in a wonderfully long, monogamous relationship. Women were always in and out of our lives. I couldn't let myself feel anything about these women. None of them have put out any effort to keep up with me, and I never felt it should have been up to me to initiate contact with them. Now most of these women are out of our lives completely. But I'm really good friends with my mom's current lover, whom she has been with over a year.

So far I've only had two boyfriends. I started being sexual fairly late, when I was nineteen. I think it was hard for me to make friends before that because we moved so much, and I've always been friends with people first before I get involved with them. When I meet guys, I tell them about my mom up front, very matter-of-factly. Neither of my boyfriends had issues about it, and both of them came from pretty straight families. Since my mother has always been a constant integral part of my life, if it's a problem for somebody, I just don't have time for them.

Part of the reason I waited so long to get involved with boys is that my grandmother was always pushing me into it. She always wanted to know if I had a boyfriend. She's interesting. Over the years she's come full circle. When I was young, she once slapped me because I said the word "feminist"—not even the word "lesbian"! But now she asks about my mother's life and lovers. She doesn't mind coming to my mother's house and staying there. It's amazing how far she has come. She's from Tennessee, and she raised my mother Catholic. She's a strong woman and has endured a lot. She is really proud of me and my life, and she realizes that my mother—despite her lesbianism—is a good mother.

When I was growing up, she would always tell me that I was pretty and that boys would surely like me. Now she wants me to have children, and I don't want to have kids. I suppose she wants what every grandmother wants, but it's an interesting battle. She stresses that she loves my mother, but she definitely doesn't want me to be like her. When I was younger these were weird messages, but now I see where she's coming from. She saw my mother's difficulty in relationships, but she never saw how her straight daughter's relations with men were similar—if not worse—than my mother's relationships.

Lesbians having children should be completely open with their kids and their sexuality. They should raise them to be open, loving people, and kids should be able to find out who they are without being pressured to think one way or another. Parents should provide positive role models, both straight and gay, so there isn't this sense of "us and them." And talking to kids is the best thing of all. Kids should be able to develop their own opinions and ideas and still feel like they are loved. I also think it's important to give kids an idea of the history and contributions of lesbians and gays. Lesbians have fought an uphill struggle, and that is important to realize. There are lesbians everywhere. All over the world, there are communities everywhere. Kids should know there are different kinds of lesbians, with different viewpoints, and different lifestyles.

Two Moms, No Hamburgers!

Carl E. Cade

I'm twelve and I live in Oakland, California. I have two mothers and I call them both mom. I have a little brother, Ojo, who is five. I really like listening to National Public Radio.

About a year ago one of my mothers moved out of the house we were all living in, and now she lives in an artist's live/work space about a mile away. My brother and I go back and forth between the two houses. It wasn't really that hard when my mothers split up. For a while it was hard to remember where I left things. And the rules are different at each house. But that was always true; my mothers have different ways of doing things. They have different ways of looking at things and different points of view. Now one of my moms is seeing someone else whom I like very much. In fact, my other mother likes this woman, too.

In one house we live with our co-parent, another mother and her seven-year-old boy, and a gay male roommate. I like going back and forth between the big house and the artist's space because the big house sometimes feels like pandemonium. And usually I'm not around a lot of men. I'm mostly around women, but I don't have a real problem with it. Our male roommate is really nice to me. He is black, and my little brother, who is half black, asked him to be his father. He said "Sure!" but I don't really think he was serious.

The first real time I realized things were different about my family was when I went to first grade. The teachers would say, "Give this to your mommy and daddy" or "Take this home to your mom and dad." To some extent, I already knew that things were different with us, but when school started is when I really understood things. At preschool there had been both kids with straight parents and lesbian parents. And at that time all my friends had lesbian parents. They lived close by, and we were friends because there was a lesbian mothers' group. Us kids were all really young, so we didn't talk about things being different about our mothers.

At my old school when I'd get sick, the nurse would say, "Who's this other person on your emergency card?" I never answered, and I hoped she'd stop asking. At my new school everybody keeps asking me things. When they see my moms, they say, "I thought that other one was your mother." One of my moms is really involved with the PTA, and the other one comes to one of my classrooms every couple of weeks. I shrug the questions off. I told one kid that one was my aunt and that I just call her my mom. My mom is not very happy about me saying that. But it's hard sometimes. I don't know what the kids would do if they knew. I don't think they'd be very upset, but maybe their parents would be. My teachers and principal know about my moms.

When I was younger, I went to women's festivals with my mother. There's this kind of famous picture of me and my biological mom. She's on this stage with long hair and her breasts are hanging out and she's got me in her arms. I always try to hide that picture, but it always finds its way back onto her desk. It's kind of embarrassing. My mother was one of the first lesbians to choose to have a child.

My mom used a donor to get pregnant, and I don't know who it is. I don't know anything about him. Right now that doesn't matter that much to me. Maybe at a later time it might be important for me to find him. For the time being it's okay. From the first time I asked, my mom always told me that I had a donor. I might have been two years old when I first asked, "Where's my daddy?" She probably said, "You don't have a daddy, you have a donor."

Almost all of the kids I know who have lesbian moms have donors. Right now I don't have any reason to find out who my donor was. He could be a real asshole. I think that was part of my mom's decision not to know the donor; he could be really awful. He could also be real nice, but it's hard to say. My brother also has a donor. People find it hard to believe we are brothers, because I am white, but I don't feel like he's my half-brother or anything.

I have a wonderful grandmother. I'm the oldest grand-son, and she treats me very special. She is my biological grandparent. My other mom's parents are kind of *almost* my grandparents. They don't approve of lesbians. They are starting to send us presents for Christmas and stuff, but just little things. I also have an aunt on that side of the family who I visit on the East Coast. She's really great. Every time I go there I am jet-lagged, so we go to the late movies and stay up really late. I also have eight cousins who live close by. I see them from time to time.

I don't think my moms are going to have more kids. I don't really want more. I like things kind of quiet. I think that if you are a child of a gay or lesbian, you have a better chance of having a great parent. If you are a lesbian, you have to go through a lot of trouble to get a child, so that child is really wanted. Everybody says that lesbians and gays have a better track record about staying together and doing a good job with kids because it's so hard to do it.

The hardest part of my life right now is that both my moms are vegetarians.

Of Lesbian Descent

Kyneret Hope

I'm twenty-five and live in Northampton, Massachusetts. I have mixed feelings about sending this out into the world, but I'm excited to see my name in print.

My mother was three months pregnant with me when she married my father. They were both very young, and they moved directly out of their orthodox Jewish parents' homes into their shared one. I was born in 1964, and my brother followed three years later. My parents' marriage lasted nine years, but I don't have any memories of them together. I do, however, remember my mother telling my brother and me that our father would be moving out of our apartment. We cried, but we didn't fully understand what changes this would bring about in our lives.

The year following my parents' separation was a full one for my mother. I remember her going through periods of depression, when she wouldn't leave her bed for days, and I remember her having some pretty wild times, too. She brought buckets of fried chicken into our formerly kosher home! And though I didn't see it with my own eyes, I knew she was riding in cars on the Shabbos. Imagine that.

During this time my mother came out as a lesbian. Her first major relationship with a woman came after she and some friends went to a concert which was only for women. One friend fell in love with the drummer, another with the bass player, and my mother with the piano player. My mother aggressively pursued this rock star, and before I knew it we had moved in with her. Her name was Linda, and she and my mother were lovers for nine years.

At that time my brother and I were still attending Jewish day school, and spending weekends and Wednesday evenings with our father. This schedule began to erode. Our mother was increasingly involved in her lesbianism and the budding lesbian separatist movement, and her development was not reconcilable with our family structure. As a result she decided to give my father custody of my brother. I think she believed she couldn't provide him with the best home possible, and that it would be better for everyone if he lived with our dad. I continued to live with our mother and to visit my father and brother at the arranged times.

That system didn't last long. I stopped attending Jewish day school, and visitations became strained. I was having trouble spending the weekdays with lesbians who discussed the evils of the patriarchy and the value of women-only space, and then spending an orthodox Shabbos with the other side of my family on the weekends. I didn't know how to make the transition without feeling like I was betraying one or the other of my parents. I would cry upon leaving my mother's, and I felt awkward in my father's community. When I returned to my mother and Linda's house, I felt I had befriended the enemy. I had to choose. I began to refuse to go to my dad's, and soon he decided to fight for my custody.

It took a little while for the case to get going, because the three of us moved from the Midwest to the East Coast, but once it did, my mother's lesbianism was of central importance. It was a long and ugly custody battle. The three of us were questioned at length, and so were teachers, psychologists, our friends and others. Though I was only eleven years old, I was asked about our home (Was it clean? Did I have my own room?), my mother's sexuality (Did she and Linda kiss in front of me? Did they share a bedroom? A bed?), and my own sexuality (Had I been to a gay bar? Was I "AC/DC?"). Occasionally the judge had to call a recess because I was crying uncontrollably, but I was tough and didn't cry very often. I wanted to appear mature and not do or say anything that might sway the judge in my father's favor.

The day the judge was to announce his verdict, the courtroom was packed. There were a lot of lesbians there. We heard later that there was also a man in the gallery who was fighting his lesbian ex-wife for custody and had come to see a lesbian lose. And lose she did. When the verdict was announced, my mother and I tried to run out of the courthouse, but everyone chased us and a huge fistfight ensued. Police officers, lawyers and lesbians were all yelling and punching each other in the lobby. One policeman held my neck in the crook of his elbow while he swung with his other arm. It's comical in retrospect. But as a result of our defiance, I wasn't even allowed to go home to collect my things. I went to the airport with my father directly from the courthouse.

I made a scene on the airplane. I cried, vomited, and conveniently lost a tooth, so I had blood all over my face. It was quite dramatic. I was shaken up, but I thought it was a good idea to publicly embarrass my father. He is generally a gentle father, and must have been appalled to find himself appearing abusive.

I spent four days at my dad's, but it felt much longer. My father's mother bought me clothes I didn't like, and my father bought me clothes I liked but couldn't wear to the religious school I was to attend. My brother resented sharing the attention he'd had to himself before I'd arrived, adding to my feeling out of place and unwelcome. I spoke to my mother and Linda every day, and my grandmother warned me that if I didn't get used to my new life, my father would get sick of me and put me in a foster home. Everyone was doing what they thought was right, but it was too much to bear. On the night of Purim, a winter Jewish holiday, I ran away while my father was getting something out of the trunk of the car. The last thing I heard was my brother saying, "There goes Kyneret."

I made it back to the East Coast with help from friends, who risked being charged with kidnaping. I started out running alone down the street, then I was driven, then I flew, and then I was driven again. I ran the last few blocks back to my mom.

Once I got home, I hid out in a motel room while the legal stuff was sorted through. It ended when we hired a lawyer who argued that my constitutional right to representation had been violated. Thus, an indefinite stay was put on the original verdict because the legal process had been invalid. We went all the way to the state Supreme Court and set a children's rights precedent. Previous to my case, only rights of parents were protected.

My mother was never granted full custody of me, and my father could have chosen to appeal the stay at any time. He didn't, but this precarious position made me insecure about having a relationship with my dad. I was afraid he would come swoop me up if he knew about the unusual way I was being raised. As a result, my father and I spoke very little and didn't see each other at all from the time of the custody case until I was eighteen years old and legally able to live on my own. He tried to maintain contact, but I shunned him. I still was unable to have relationships with both sides of my family without feeling I was betraying one or the other of them, as well as threatening my living situation. So I forfeited my dad in order to maintain a more stable and calm life. I also lost contact with my brother during those years.

As time went on, my mother and Linda were more and more separatist in their orientation. When I started fourth grade in our local public school, they notified the principal and the teachers that they were lesbians. Subsequently I was placed in classes much below my level. I was in a reading group with kids who were struggling to read "fire hydrant," and then going home to read *Rubyfruit Jungle,* the lesbian primer novel. I was quickly transferred to a liberal private school, largely on a scholarship. Though the people at the new school were also aware that I was being raised by lesbians, it wasn't nearly as much of an issue there as it had been at the other school.

I went back to public school for junior high. By then, things were very bad at home. As Linda says now, she and my mother had unrealistic expectations of me. My mother now says the situation was emotionally abusive. I was criticized for being messy, for leaving any mark of my presence around the apartment, and for not articulately expressing my feelings. My friendships were controlled: I was discouraged from having male friends, and any female friends were to be made aware that I lived in a lesbian household before I could have them over.

Because of this time in my life, I have come to associate separatism with a certain edge of hardness that permeated our home. It is difficult to admit—I was raised on the stuff and am very defensive of separatism as a valuable part of the growth of many individual lesbians and of the community. But I experienced separatism as a constant level of anger and negativity. Separatism, as I appreciate it, comes from loving in others what you love about yourself—or what you are learning to love about yourself. That was part of the lifestyle I knew, but there was also a down side: men were called mutants, straight women were considered disowned sisters who wasted woman-energy on men, and other lesbians were sometimes accused of being government spies sent to infiltrate and undermine the community. Anyone who was not like us was evil, and I had to be careful not to cross over to the enemy's camp.

Separatism wasn't our only problem. No matter what the causes, by the time I was fourteen, our family was in an awful mess. I moved out and went to live in a lesbian boarding house about a block from my school. The boarding house on Green Street was a good place for me to make the transition from my mother's house to being on my own. My housemates treated me as an equal, but they took extra care of me because I was still a kid.

One of the many wonderful things about being the daughter of a lesbian is that I was given the opportunity to be part of a strong lesbian community. Lesbians, now all over the country, have watched me grow since I was ten years old, and have nurtured me when my mother couldn't. They have become my extended family.

I lived on Green Street for nearly four years and was immersed in the lesbian community. I earned a living by working at the women's restaurant, and for recreation,

I studied and taught karate at the women's martial arts school. My life was split into two very distinct segments: my lesbian friends knew nothing about school, and my school friends didn't know where I lived or worked. Partly I was afraid my father would fight for custody again if he somehow heard how I was living, but I also wanted to maintain a ruse at school that I was like everybody else. Not only didn't I have a mom and a dad in a house with a washer and dryer, I also felt like a fraudulent member of teenage society. I wasn't familiar with their social mores, I didn't understand their relationships, and boys were an enigma to me.

There came a point when I decided, for the sake of my growth and my health, to shift the focus of my life onto my peer group. During the summer between my junior and senior years of high school, I moved, quit karate, and changed jobs. I did a lot at once. I even started dating boys. I'd had girlfriends before, but never anything with a boy. In one night I had my first straight date and ate a hamburger after being a vegetarian for six years. What a night! The burger didn't make me ill—neither did the boy.

Since that summer in 1981 I have spent a lot of time trying to understand my peers, and still this remains unfinished. I've become more like them, though. I even do some of the incomprehensible things they do, which is comforting. Nonetheless, one result of my upbringing is that though I have a strong sense of community, I don't foresee ever having that feeling of walking into a group and thinking, "These people are like me. Finally I feel among my own." I'm at ease in many settings, but I retain a sense of being different. As I grow up I see this feeling is not unique to me—everyone feels like an anthropologist observing a foreign culture sometimes. Maybe I just feel that way more often than most. The residual effects of having been involved in so many contradictory fringe groups (separatists, orthodox Jews, self-supporting teens, etc.) are hard to amalgamate.

It was with the goal of integrating the seemingly incompatible sides of me that I recently moved back to my hometown after being away for about six years. I now live three blocks from Green Street, half a block from Linda's office, and eight blocks from my mother's house. It is timely that I am writing this retrospective here and now. I'm trying to wrap up the past and move on, and that process is stirring up a mess I hadn't realized needed to be sorted through.

I have learned so many diverse lessons from the way I grew up. I have learned to value humor and communication, and to believe that with these tools and my intelligence I can do anything. I was always told I was smart and special. Lesbians encouraged me to be proud and female.

I also learned to fear the world's judgment, to see relationships as temporary, to be distrustful, and to withhold communication as a means of self-protection and punishment. A lot of these lessons come from being raised by people at odds with their surroundings. Others came from losing my father, brother and then my mother as a primary caretaker for a while, even though I now have them all back in my life. When I read over what I've written, I see evidence of how emotionally detached I've become. I coped with the turmoil of my childhood by shutting off my feelings, and this shows. I can't go back now and add the appropriate sentimental responses to various events—I didn't feel anything when most of this story was happening.

There is one lesson I wish I'd learned from lesbians but didn't. With all the powerful influences in my life that have tried to counteract society's sexism and homophobia, it perplexes me how much of that garbage I've swallowed. I am sexist and homophobic in that it's-okay-for-them-but-not-for-me way. I'm amazed at myself. Being raised by big beautiful women, why do I still think I'm fat and ugly—to the point of occasionally flirting with anorexia? And when I was involved with a woman, why did I panic to hear the word "lesbian" used about me? "Lesbian" doesn't accurately describe my lifestyle or sexuality, but why did it scare me like that? I'm very disturbed by this. How did it happen? Shouldn't I be different?

I remember a conversation with Linda and my mother from my youth in which they explained their parenting style by saying that the patriarchy was pushing me hard in one direction, and they wanted to counteract that pressure by pushing just as hard in the other. I'm lucky I didn't get squashed. I ended up resenting both constraining forces, and was left with no appealing role models. I haven't known who or what to strive to become.

My unhealthy body image comes at least partially from thinking I have to be society's definition of "the ideal woman" on the outside, because I'm so far from it on the inside. As to the homophobia, my mother has helped me by pointing out that I have seen an ugly side of lesbianism and societal oppression of lesbians—why wouldn't I be afraid of it? She also helps me absolve myself of the responsibility of being the golden daughter of the lesbian community. I can be a little sexist and homophobic like everyone else. I don't have to be perfect. Besides, she thinks I'm perfect just the way I am.

My mother! She is who she is because she's a lesbian, and she is precious to me. When I have kids, I hope to do some things differently than she did, but I imagine I'll make other mistakes in their places. I hope, like my mother, I can make my relationship with my children as unconditionally loving and dynamic as ours.

The combination of a Jewish and lesbian heritage has served me well. I have to laugh, though, when I imagine what the complete family gathering would include: black-hat-and-bearded rabbi meets radical lesbian CPA, lesbian Hindu monk meets orthodox yeshiva boy. My rich cultural background is exemplified by the combination of people who would show up at such a party. I love my family! But what would I wear?

Telling It Like It Is

Rachel Liana Rothman

I'm fifteen years old and live in Florida. I love acting and I play softball. For most of my life, I lived half with my mom and half with my dad. Last year I spent six months in Israel with my dad, and since I've come back I have lived full time with my mom. I was nine when my mother came out to me.

I have a problem; well, it's not really a problem, but it's something that affects me. My mom's gay. She's a lesbian. Yeah, yeah, big deal, right? Well, yeah, it is. To me anyways.

Sometimes I feel like no one really knows what I'm going through; either that, or that they don't acknowledge that this thing with my mom is a big deal for me. Like if I'm having a hard time dealing with my mom and what she does, some of her friends will think I'm being ridiculous. They're like my second family, but sometimes they just don't understand that having a mom who is a lesbian is not an everyday thing for most people.

Wait a sec—it's not always like this all the time or anything. I mean, most of the time it's really great. It's only when my mom embarrasses me or when my friends—or maybe I should say the people at school—give me a hard time that this is difficult.

Sometimes I feel like my mom really looks different, like she doesn't look like other moms to me. It's the way she dresses. I feel like lesbianism just reeks off her even when I know it really doesn't. But it's still hard. And then there are all the bumper stickers on her car, not lesbian ones, but "Fight Racism," "Peace and Justice" and stuff like that. Other people don't have that stuff on their cars. And there are all these buttons in the living room, that say stuff like "ERA Now" and "Why Be Normal?" and "I'm the one your mother warned you about." My school friends—like *guys*—come over and just look at them like, *What the hell?*

Don't get me wrong, I really do love my mom and all her friends, but being gay is just not acceptable to other people. Like at school, people make jokes about dykes and fags, and it really bothers me. I mean I bite my tongue, because if I say anything, they wonder, Why is she sticking up for them? But my close friends love my mom and think she's great. A lot of them like coming and talking with her if they have a problem because she's so open and easy to talk to.

But then there are the hard times, like when my mom had a lover move in with us, one that I did not like. They're not together anymore, but when they were I tried to make life hell for them. Her lover was totally invading my space and she expected to just fit right in. I was like: No, this is not your house! And then it was especially hard to have someone else important in my mother's life besides me. Before, I was always the only one.

Another thing that made me mad was that her lover didn't respect my feelings at all about being out. I mean she was *really* out, she had lesbian bumper stickers all over her car, and she looked like a dyke! I couldn't stand it when she would try to hug my mom in front of my friends! When she lived with us I fought constantly with her. Once I told my mom that she'd have to choose between me and her lover or else I'd live with my dad. She said she wished I wouldn't make her do that. I couldn't believe that she didn't just say, "Oh, of course I'd choose you."

Now it was one thing for her lover to move in with us, but it was another thing for her to go on the Oprah Winfrey show and come out to the whole world without telling me first. That's how all my friends found out about her and my mom. A few of my guy friends were watching the show over at my best friend's house. And just by accident they saw her. They had met her, but they thought she was our "roommate." After the show they put two and two together. Then it got all over school. That must have been one of the worst experiences of my life. People teased me and stuck mean notes in my locker that said some really mean and hurtful things.

Want an example? Here, how about this:

DAUGHTERS
OF
LESBIAN
LOVERS

Do you have any idea how that makes a teenager like me feel? To put it bluntly: like shit. I didn't tell my mom about this, because I guess things were so bad at home, and I didn't want to make things worse. I was afraid of what she would feel. Because of *her* these people were being mean to me. I could not believe my mom's lover went on the show. She didn't even tell me she was going to be on it! It really messed up my life. I swear to god, that woman has some nerve.

Then, after they broke up, my mother saw this woman who was really amazing. She told my mom that she didn't know what to wear the first time that we were going to meet. She asked my mom what she thought I would like her to wear! Stuff like that makes me feel like she really cared about me and my feelings.

And then there is my dad; he really hates my mom. When we were in Israel and I was really missing my mom, he wouldn't even let me call home even though I was *really* homesick. I wanted to go home, but my dad's wife said that one reason they didn't want me to come back early was because they thought that if I was with my mom full time I would grow up "to be like her." Give me a break! It's not like lesbianism is contagious. They said their family was a "real family" and they could provide me with "a stable environment." But I don't like them or like living with them. Me and my dad clash; our chemistry just does not mix. He doesn't like me or anything I do.

I'm in an acting improvisation class, and I did a monologue about my mom, and her coming out to me and what it was like. My dad came to see the performance. In it I say stuff about my father and how hard it is when he and his wife say bad things about my mom. The last line is, "I love you, daddy, and I'm sorry if I hurt you, but you've hurt me too, a lot." After the show he came up and hugged me, but I went to his house four days later and he didn't even say one word to me about it. It was like it didn't happen or something. We are supposed to tour with the show, to high schools and community centers, but I'm not sure I would be able to perform at my own high school. People would say, "She's not acting, that stuff is true."

But things with my mother's ex-lover and with my dad are never going to change the way I feel about my mom. She has given me so much. Probably a lot more than some straight mothers have. She's so open and loving. She still tucks me in at night and even sings me my favorite lullaby if I want her to! Now how many fifteen-year-old kids can say that? She's not perfect—far from it!—but she's my mom and I love her.

Overcoming Fear

Jafar

I'm ten years old and I like baseball. My favorite subject is math. I like people from around the world from different cultures. I like to talk to them. I am black and I have friends of all different colors.

My mom tried to break things to me easy. I kind of freaked out and was pretty upset. I was nine. Actually, I really flipped out. I wasn't sure I was going to be able to like her and live with her as a regular mom like before. I thought being a lesbian was weird. I felt like living with my dad for a little while. I overcame my feelings, and then when I came back to my mom, I wasn't that scared anymore. She's still a great mom. She supports me and makes dinner for me, and if I'm sick she takes care of me. If my throat is really sore she'll make me soup, even if I can't talk and tell her that's what I would want. She figures it out because she always knows what I like.

As I started to know what a lesbian was, it became easier for me to become her son again, and easier for her to become my mother again. We worked stuff out. One day we went to a lesbian restaurant and my mom and I got a table. We ate breakfast. We were enjoying ourselves, and then she asked me why I was so upset and didn't talk to her anymore. I told her I was freaked out. She told me there was no reason for me to freak out, but I could if I wanted to. I cried a little and sat next to her and ordered something to drink, and she talked to me some more. We went home that night and the next day I said, "Mom, I love you even if you are a lesbian," and then I gave her a nice long hug.

My mom has had four different girlfriends and I got to know them all. It was difficult to know the first three girlfriends, and I didn't get to know them all that much. Her last girlfriend has stayed with her a long time, so it's been easier to hold onto her. This woman is like my friend. Lesbian women are just the same as other women.

I've never talked to my dad about any of this. It just stays between me and my mom. My dad doesn't know that my mom is a lesbian. I think it would bother him. Maybe he knows but he doesn't talk about it.

I think if kids at school found out about my mom, they would tease me. Some of the kids at school would tease you even if they didn't know what a lesbian was.

I went to the gay and lesbian parade. I saw men in women's costumes and women in men's costumes. It was weird. This made me confused. I haven't asked my mom about it. Also there was a fire engine at the parade and there was a sign on it that said that gays and lesbians could be as good firefighters as anybody on the planet. There was also a police car with a picture of two men on it and two women on it. The men were partners and the ladies were partners, too.

Sometimes I feel happy and sometimes I feel sad. Sometimes I get sad for her being a lesbian, and sometimes I wish she was a regular mom, my old mom. She is the same mom, but I have a feeling like she's different now.

Sometimes I talk to my mom about this. We just lie there on the bed and look off into the future and wonder what is going to happen to her and me. We talk about what happens to us. We try to see what will happen to us. I see me growing up as a baseball player. And I see my mom getting older and living with her girlfriend Margaret for a long time.

It wasn't fun for me to find out my mom was a lesbian. If other kids find out their mom is a lesbian, they should know it is okay to freak out. I'd say to these kids: Be scared, but try to talk to your mom about it. See if you can work out something. Let your mom be helpful to you. My mom told me that it was okay to cry and okay to be afraid. But talk to your mom. Let her help you overcome your fears.

Home Is Where . . .

Ishana Dolly Elizabeth Strazzero Wild

I am seven. Ishana is my Indian name and it means pride. Dolly is because I was a little doll when I was little. My mom's last name is Strazzero and my other mom's last name is Wild. My sister's name is Asha.

I'm adopted and I'm from India. I don't care where I'm from, but I want to go visit there someday. When I'm twelve I'm going there. I take Indian dancing classes. My teacher is very stern. If you don't do it right, you can't be in the performance. Once I went to my teacher's house and danced for some other Indian people.

Sometimes I feel funny about looking different from my mothers, but I know I love them and they love me, even though I'm a different color. I kind of miss the home where I was before coming here, because I never really got to see it. I came here when I was about a month old. And other people don't care that I'm a different color. They just want to know if I'm nice. Last night I got to sleep over at my friend's house. She likes me even though she's white and she's Jewish.

My family is Lizzie, my mother, and Zenya, my other mother. I also have two grandmothers, and an uncle. And there is Ann, who is Lizzie's lover. And I have cousins.

I live with Lizzie sometimes, and Zenya other times. There's a schedule that says when we sleep where. We stay with Zenya Sunday till Wednesday. Then we stay with Lizzie the rest of the time. Sometimes I stay with Ann. At all the places I am always with my sister Asha. Sometimes all the moving gets confusing. I call both Lizzie and Zenya "mommy."

I used to have two lesbian mothers, but now I only have one. When we were little girls, Zenya and Lizzie lived together. They got divorced when we were two because they were always fighting. Zenya has a boyfriend now, and he doesn't treat us very good. Sometimes he tells us what to do and makes us sit in the back seat in the car when we go places.

It makes me sad. Now we don't have as much fun. Because Zenya isn't a lesbian anymore, when we are with her we don't get to go to any of the lesbian dances, and all my best friends are there. I love to go to the lesbian dances. Some people think it's strange to see women dancing together. There was a show on TV with this man saying that lesbians shouldn't have rights. I thought he was wrong. I like lesbians. It's fair if people want to be lesbian.

I told some of my best friends about having a lesbian mom and they said, "You have a lesbian mom!" They are so surprised. They all have dads. I like having two moms because my friends get spanked by their daddies. I say that daddies are dumb as bubble gum! I like Lizzie being with Ann because I get to snuggle with them in the nighttime.

I think in a family you need enough love, and enough

food and enough clothes and enough toys. I like having a sister, but she bites me sometimes. When she starts fighting, I start talking about my feelings, but she keeps fighting.

I want to be a doctor or a veterinarian when I grow up. I don't know if I want to be a lesbian. I might like men. I might get married. I might not like men. I might be a lesbian. I might like to be with both. I don't really know yet. There are a lot of choices.

. . . Where
the Heart is!

*Asha Rani
Catherine
Wild Strazzero*

*Rani means Queen
in Indian and Asha
means Hope. I was
adopted, which means
that I didn't come out
of my mother. I've seen
pictures of India where
I come from, and all the
people there are brown-
skinned. Brown is my
favorite color because I
love chocolate and
chocolate is brown.
I am seven.*

I live in Massachusetts and there are woods nearby. I
have five cats and three dogs and eight chickens.
When I was a little girl my two moms were lovers; then
they broke up. Then Zenya fell in love with someone
else. Now Lizzie is lovers with Ann.

Zenya is lovers with a man, but she says she might
break up because he isn't nice to us. We have talked to
her about it, and she told us she cares about us more
than she does for him. He doesn't let us join in conversations. Ann always lets us join in conversations because
she really likes us. We've known her since we were two.

All my friends know I have two moms, but some of them think that one of them is my mom and one of them is my sister's mom. But that's not true. Both of them are my moms. Most people understand. But one boy said it's not right to have a lesbian mom. He said my mother should be married and I should have a father. But I don't want to have a father.

I like having a sister, but we are separated in class now and I don't like that. My grandmother's not a lesbian, but she came to one of the lesbian dances. She said she felt a little bit funny about it. We told her that if she wanted to go home because she didn't want to be with lesbians, that was okay. But it seemed like she had a little bit of fun.

One of my mommies lives up the road; my sister and I go back and forth between houses. Some weekends we are at one mommy's, and sometimes we are at the other. When we were little we used to have to go back and forth and back and forth all the time, but now we stay at each house longer and it's much better. It used to be exhausting.

I maybe want to be a dentist someday, but I don't know if I want to be a lesbian.

Stuff Like That

Megan

I'm fifteen and my mother and father are both gay. I live with my mother, Darcy, and brother, Jim, in Lansing, Michigan, and I visit my father every other weekend. I love sports and I'm a fast-pitch softball pitcher for my high school team.

I don't remember when my dad first told me he was gay. I think it was right after the divorce, but I always remember him as gay. I didn't understand it at first. He had lived with the same man for over nine years, and I grew up thinking, "Hey, they're roommates and best friends and that kind of stuff." But then, when my mom told me a few years ago that she was gay, too, it sort of popped into my head what he had meant.

My mom came out to me a few days after her birthday. She had gone out that night and met her first woman lover, Carmen. She just sat me down and started talking to me and telling me that she was gay and stuff like that. I was surprised. It kind of freaked me out at first. My reaction was, "Oh, no, not you, too," because it made me think about my dad.

I walked around and thought about it a lot. It caught me off guard, and was kind of scary to hear. It's so different from the normal thing, from other kids. I talked to my mom about it, but I didn't talk to anyone else at that point.

After my mom told me about herself, I met Carmen. After a while I got used to them being lovers, and Carmen and I got along pretty good together.

My mom was a lot happier after she came out, and she and Carmen were together about four months. It was hard for me when my mom told me they were breaking up, because I liked Carmen. Me and Carmen are still really close friends, and I see her every once in a while. I saw her at the Michigan Womyn's Music Festival and spent some time with her. My mom and her are still pretty good friends.

After Carmen and my mom broke up, my mom dated for a long time. Then she started seeing Nancy. She was with her for about three years, and Nancy and her son— who was about the same age as I was—lived with us for over a year. Nancy and I didn't get along too well. We liked each other, but I didn't get close to her. Her son was a real jerk, a male chauvinist, and he didn't want to accept my mom and Nancy being together. He treated my mom pretty badly, and Nancy took it out on me. Nancy was with another woman before my mom, and when her son and my mom got into a fight, he'd say, "I wish my mom was still with [the other woman]."

My mom told me that she and Nancy broke up partly because of us kids, but also because of them. I guess I understand what my mom meant. Sometimes I wish we had gotten along better, but Nancy really didn't make any effort to talk to me.

Because I didn't get really close to Nancy, that wasn't a hard breakup for me. But there was one woman that I was really close to, and when my mom broke up with her, it was really hard. That was when I decided not to get so close to mom and dad's lovers. Now, I just take my time getting close to women my mom is dating. My mom used to say things to me about it, but now she understands what I'm doing. My brother does the same thing. He is really, *really* close to my dad's ex, and he hasn't gotten really close to any of my dad's lovers since—or my mom's lovers, either.

When they bring somebody new home for us to meet, it feels kind of weird. I'm really quiet the first few times. I don't really talk much and try to go someplace on my bike after dinner. I don't mind if they ask me how old I am, or where I go to school, or stuff like that. But if they ask things that are personal, I get uncomfortable. Like one of them asked me if I was gay like my mom. I didn't answer her.

My mom isn't seeing anyone right now, but my dad has been seeing the same guy for about a year. The man is married, so he doesn't live with my dad. I don't know what's going to happen, but my dad's ex is moving back from New York, and I'm hoping they will get back together. I used to be able to talk with him really good. He'd understand things that my dad would do and explain them to my brother and me. He was really close to my brother, and my brother is really happy that he's moving back here to Michigan.

The bad thing about my mom or my dad living with someone is that it doesn't seem like my brother and I have any say about how it feels. It's just sort of up to them. They ask us how we feel about someone, and they listen, but, yet, they don't. They do what they want anyway. At first when my parents got divorced, I used to wish they would live together again. I think that most kids want that when their parents are divorced. Before I knew about my mom, I used to ask why they couldn't live together. But now, I don't really want that anymore. Ever since my mom's been a lesbian, she's been a lot happier.

I don't think the rest of my family really minds about my mom and dad being gay. My great-grandma lived with us four of the five years my parents were married, and then she lived with my brother, mom and me for three years when I was nine, ten, and eleven, too. She and I are close, but I've never talked to her about my parents. It's just sort of understood. She accepts it, kind of, but then she doesn't, too. I think she wishes mom wasn't gay, but she is close to mom and glad that she is happier now that she's out.

I haven't told many of my friends about my parents being gay. I think I've told three. Patty, who used to be my best friend, knew because I told her, and the other two just kind of asked me about it. They guessed, because my mom didn't see any guys and I never talked about her having boyfriends or anything. When I told them, they just said, "Oh, that's cool." We only talked about it a couple of times.

Me and my mom told Patty together. She was really close to my mom, and she even called her "mom." She was fine with it, but her mom is pretty weird, so she didn't tell her about my mom for the longest time. Patty didn't want me and her not to be able to see each other. When she finally told her mom, she actually was fine about it.

I think it's easier that both my parents are gay than it would be if just one of them was gay. Sometimes, though, it's hard having two gay parents, because I can't really talk to anybody about it. But I have a lot of grown-up gay friends. I can talk to them about my mom or about anything in my life.

I used to think it would be pretty weird to be gay, but now I know it's just the same. It's just love, even if it's two women loving each other or two men loving each other. Gay people are just as good as straight people, and they can be just as good parents.

Sometimes there are advantages to my parents being gay. I can relate really good to my mom. I can't talk to my dad real well, and right now I don't know that much about his life. I'm just finding out stuff that I've never known about him. But I'm really close to my mom.

I think I am more open-minded than if I had straight parents. Sometimes kids at school make a big deal out of being gay. They say it's stupid and stuff like that. But they don't really know, because they are not around it. I don't say anything to them, but I know they are wrong. I get kind of mad, because they don't know what they are talking about.

Sometimes I think about being gay. At first, I thought my mom would love me more if I was gay. But when we talked about it, she said she'd love me the same whatever I was. So that doesn't really bother me anymore. I guess if I was gay, everyone would blame it on my mom and dad. But I don't think they would be right. My mom was telling me the other day that my grandma and grandpa were saying they were worried about me turning out gay. My mom told them it was going to be my choice.

I guess I'm straight right now. I don't really know how old you have to be to know you're gay. I guess it's just when you know that's what you are. My mom said she knew when she was a little girl, and my dad said he's known for a long time.

I would say I'm a feminist. I'm interested in learning about everything. My mom is telling me the political parts of things. I read books about it, too. I'm learning about women's rights and how we always have to fight for them. I've gone to the Take Back the Night and the Gay Pride marches.

Most of the adults I know are gay, like the women on the women's softball team I hang out with. I feel pretty comfortable with them, probably more comfortable than if I was walking around with friends from school. They call me "the community kid" because I'm close to a lot of people. It's fun. I call them up and talk, or ride my bike around and visit, and maybe go out to dinner with them.

I think if I was gay and I had a kid, I'd tell them right away about being gay. I don't think it's the kind of thing you should keep from your kid. Not telling them is like excluding them from your life. I think you have to be twelve or thirteen to really understand it; that's when it really sunk in for me. I'd also tell them they don't have to be gay, that it is their choice and not to let anyone pressure them.

I think my mom is a real good mom. And even if she was straight, she'd be the same mom. The thing that matters is how mothers teach kids, and how they influence them. They should be willing to teach you about things, but not really tell you what to do with your life.

Live and
Let Live

Jon Dylan

I'm thirteen and I write poetry. I'm getting published in my school newspaper and I'm very excited about it. I live in Oklahoma City.

The funny thing is that right now there's a rumor going around at school that my mom's a lesbian and that there are naked women hanging all around our house. A girl heard me talk about my mom being gay in an Ala-teen meeting, and she must have talked, because it got around. When people ask me about it, I say, "Hell, no! My mom's not a lesbian! Shut your face!" and stuff like that. Meanwhile, my friends have been supporting me. Actually it depends on who is asking as to what I say. Sometimes I'm more shy. No one at school knows one hundred percent sure that my mom is gay and I haven't told them. I am shy about my mom and her lover being seen together, but because they are so much together, I think people will suspect. Right now I tell people that they are "best friends."

I guess I always knew about my mom, but when I really figured it out I was in kindergarten. This guy approached me and asked me about my mom hugging and kissing the woman that she lived with. I clammed up. When he said she was gay, I said, "Uh-uh, no way." I went home and my mom explained to me what being a lesbian was and what a great responsibility it was for me to know that she was a lesbian.

My mom has told me about what happened to Harvey Milk, the gay politician in San Francisco who was shot, and she said that teachers had been threatened with losing their jobs if they were gay. She is a teacher at my school. She also told me that she knows how really hard it is for me to be pro-gay in my society of teenagers.

My mom has a lover now, and it really doesn't bother me because now I'm letting my mother live her own life, and she lets me live mine. My mom's lover is nice; she's a professional. We stay at her house on the weekends. They do a lot of hugging, touching and kissing. I think it's the same thing to see her kiss her lover as it would be if my dad was kissing a girl.

Homosexuality really doesn't bother me. I know a lot of gay people, some who are my mom's friends. Once I was with a friend of mine and there was this guy who talked in a real high voice and he was playing soccer. My friend called him a fag, and I couldn't stand it. I walked off. We talked later and I told him that prejudice make me sick. He said, "I'm not prejudiced." I said, "Yeah, you are against gays." And he said, "That's because it's not natural." So I asked him what wasn't natural about it. I told him there were gay whales and gay horses, and even gay goldfish. But he told me that the Bible says it is unnatural. So I asked him to show me where exactly in the Bible it said it was wrong.

We were at his house then, so his mom showed me some Bible verses, but I couldn't really see that any of them said anything very bad. There was something about "wantonness" and "untrue love." So I told him gay people were brighter and more accepting than most other people are, because most gay people I know are pretty talented and above the ordinary. He said it still wasn't right. He used to be one of my closest friends, but he's sure not any more.

My mom has brought me up very open-mindedly; she's very liberal. She is also a feminist. Does being a lesbian and a feminist go together? I don't know. My mom has gone to a few protests. She went to one about people with AIDS; they were demanding more action on that issue.

I love my mom, and I don't care what she chooses to be. She loves me, and I think she cares what I choose. I think she would like me to be straight. But there's this slogan that says "Live and Let Live" because whether you are black or white or gay or straight, there's no difference. People are people. It's like in that song that Holly Near sings, "We are gay and straight together, we are singing for our lives." I'm just not a prejudiced person.

Homosexuality has never been forced upon me or even suggested. But my mom wants grandchildren. She's not going to have another child, so I guess I'm her only chance. And I am quite straight. I like girls very much. Right now I'm in love with this junior from another school. Her name is Rheesy and she's got blond hair. So in no way am I gay or anything like that.

When someone calls me a fag, I don't really consider it an insult. I'm more upset that *they* consider it an insult. I wonder if they think their manlyhood is so great and if that's why they call people fags?

My life's pretty normal, but I'm weird. Being a poet is the main thing in my life. I'm a lot like my mom; she's also a poet. I look like her and sometimes talk like her. We have a lot of the same ideals.

Living with
A Secret

Denise

I'm twenty-one years old, black, and originally from New York City. Currently I'm a senior at Harvard/Radcliffe, where I'm studying psychology.

O ne night when I was seven, my mother called me and Tommy, my brother, into her bedroom. We saw Anne—the woman who had moved into our apartment two weeks before—lying next to mother in the queensize bed. Mother rolled onto her side and said, "I want you to know that Anne and I are lesbians. That means that I'm married to Anne the way I used to be married to your father. But you can't tell anyone about this because no one will understand." We told her that we understood and kissed them goodnight.

After mother came out to us, life got interesting. Anne took us fishing and camping and taught us how to use the CB in her van. Mother had a night job from Sunday to Thursday. Every Friday morning, she brought her friends home from work and had a party. Every Friday morning we ate pizza, burgers, and homemade bread for breakfast!

All of mother's friends, few of whom were heterosexual,

loved us immediately. I learned that homosexuals and lesbians are loving people who really know how to have fun. One of mother's lovers was a witch who owned an occult bookstore. She gave me a book of potions and spells. She gave mother a six-foot pyramid that saved her dying plants when they were placed inside. Mother made us sit in the pyramid whenever we were hyperactive.

Most lesbian couples we knew stayed together between three to five years. Mother could never stay tied down that long. She changed lovers every year to eighteen months. We moved a lot because mother always lived with her lovers. Mother broke my heart as well as her lover's every time she terminated a relationship. Mother said she did it for us. Each new lover had more money than her predecessor. I hated that. I loved all but one of mother's lovers. We usually lived with her lovers, and they were our primary providers. I hated the fact that mother was doing this thing that hurt me so that I could have more food to eat and better clothes to wear. Despite her changing her relationship as lovers, these women remained friends with both my mother and us kids.

I've always considered mother's sexuality to be her most admirable quality. It's also her most frustrating. Mother's friends showed me a world of laughter and caring about which I wanted to tell my friends and family. But I never did. When I was a kid, I didn't tell anyone because mother had said not to. I eventually learned that what mother meant to say in her coming-out speech was that we couldn't tell anyone about her sexuality because no one would approve.

The older I got, the more I saw that society regarded homosexuality as an unnatural thing. I didn't understand why. Homosexuals were just people expressing their love for each other—what was unnatural about that?

But mother felt guilty for making us live a secretive

life. Every year she apologized for being a lesbian, for making us keep her secret, and for changing lovers like shelf paper. That was the only time of year we saw mother cry. All three of us cried. The annual apologies stopped when we stopped living with mother—twelve years ago.

When I was nine, a representative of the Florida State Juvenile Court came to my school and asked Tommy and me questions about mother and her "roommate." By the nature of the questions, I could tell that they knew the truth about mother and wanted us to confirm it. We did what any streetwise kids would do in that situation— we lied. When mother found out that Juvenile had interrogated us, she told us it wasn't safe for us to live with her anymore because the court thought that her sexuality made her an unfit mother. We flew back to our father in New York that night and have lived with him ever since, visiting mother for three weeks every summer.

As much as I loved New York and was glad to be back (Florida is a very boring state), I missed mother's friends and their close-knit world in which I felt safe. I kept no secrets from any of them. In New York, it seemed that everyone Tommy and I knew regarded homosexuals and lesbians with disgust. Even though mother was a thousand miles away, we could easily have become the butt of everyone's insults and jokes. In fact, this is exactly what happened to me in high school.

The summer before I went to boarding school, mother told me that she hoped Tommy and I were heterosexual, because gay life was too hard. In the middle of my first year at boarding school—tenth grade—I developed a physical attraction for my roommate. I had just learned what it meant to be gay or lesbian—it took me that long to understand the sexual aspect. I panicked. I wrote in my journal about my attraction and my strong fear that I might be a lesbian just like mother. I called mother, and she told me it was just a phase, that it would pass in time. She was right. Time passed as did my infatuation. Everything was fine until the middle of April, when my roommate read that entry of my journal to every girl in our hallway.

At fifteen-and-a-half I learned the meaning of the word persecution; I lived with it every day for two months. Nasty words were written on my walls. Obscene pictures were taped to my door. Melted Jell-O was put in my bed. Through all of this, not a word was said about my mother. I did everything but threaten their lives to assure that not one derogatory remark was made about her. They didn't even make a "like mother, like daughter" wisecrack. I was "Denise the dyke" and that was it.

The following year all that stopped, because I made sure the entire school believed I was straight. I was so convincing, even I believed it. Since my ex-roommate and her following never mentioned my mother in their antics, no one else in school knew about her. I kept it that way for obvious reasons.

It was hard living with that secret, having to monitor everything I said about mother, and lying most of the time. Mother was not the only one in the closet. I was in there with her. Imagine my frustration when I couldn't convince my teacher and classmates that homosexuals should be allowed to adopt children because they are as capable of loving and raising children as heterosexuals. No one believed me because I couldn't answer their asinine question, "How would you feel if your mother was a lesbian?"

I finally started telling my friends about mother two years ago. I couldn't keep it in anymore, and I was no longer in danger of Juvenile coming to get me. So I took my chances with my friends. I'm glad I did. Most of them think it's no big deal, which is fine with me.

This summer I realized that I am bisexual. I don't know if living with my mother had influence on this or not. Mother's reaction to the news was not pleasant: "Every hair on my head is white, and I'm about to put a knife through my heart. Why, Denise? This is my fault," she said. "After observing me all those years, you're following my example."

I tried to assure her I was bisexual—not a lesbian— but she doesn't believe that bisexuality is possible. She thinks bisexuals are experimenting, and eventually they go to one side or the other. "It takes a strong person to be gay," she told me. "You can't tell anyone about this; you'll lose all your friends."

I was mad at mother for not being supportive of my decision to come out. I was mad at her for implying that I wasn't strong enough to handle bisexual life. I was mad at her for not taking my sexual orientation seriously. And I'm still mad at her now.

Mother was wrong about being unable to tell my friends. Almost all of them know, and they don't feel uncomfortable around me. After her initial reaction, mother didn't protest anymore, but she hasn't told any of her friends. I'm not sure whether it's because she thinks it's none of their business or because she's ashamed of me.

Growing up with mother was never easy, but it was never boring, either. Mother's friends and lovers were my family. They were there to comfort me after my nightmare in high school. They cheered when I got into Harvard. There's nothing they wouldn't do for me, and there's nothing I wouldn't do for them. As for mother, I love her. I've always loved her, but it's going to take me a long time to overcome the anger I feel for her right now.

My Brother's Keeper

Lise Solomon   *Since graduating from Hampshire College in 1988, I have been living in the Boston area and working at a publishing company.*

I don't remember the conversation, but as the story goes, when my mom told me and my younger brother that she was a lesbian (I must have been nine, my brother seven), our reaction was along the lines of, "So what? You kiss a man, you kiss a woman; what's the big deal?" For the most part, I think we feel that way still; however, I know that most of my brother's friends don't know, nor will they ever, and almost all of my friends do know. I try to get him to talk about it with me, I mean about our mom having been in a relationship with a woman for the last fourteen years, but he won't often talk about it in detail.

The last time we talked about it, he told me that not many of his friends knew about mom, and that when "the guys" casually call people dyke or fag, he generally participates, and doesn't confront them with the inappropriateness or seriousness of their labeling. He said he doesn't feel bad or even think much about it. I think he feels that he can call someone a fag because he doesn't do it out of ignorance or maliciousness. It bothered me to hear him so cavalierly say that it was easy for him to participate in that kind of name calling. I've been in plenty of situations where "dyke" and "fag" were being thrown around, and it wasn't until I was in college that I could disarm people who threw around those threatening words, by telling them how insulted I was because my mother was a lesbian. They would always try to back out of it and say they were just using it innocently, that they had no idea. I just walked away. So to hear my brother say that he let this go on around him—while it didn't surprise me, it did bother me. I suppose it annoyed me in part because it exposed and reminded me of times when I felt like I wouldn't fit in or be accepted if people found out about my different-ness, that was really my mother's different-ness, but a different-ness it seemed we had to take on as ours. But to my brother, I cannot say, "How can you participate?" because I have a feeling that it may be his way of getting even with her for having made him live with secrecy.

I remember the awkwardness in high school and wanting to believe that I was not different. Neither my brother nor I had many friends sleep over at our house during those high school years because it would mean explaining things. Now, just a bit beyond college, I use my mother's life choice as a way to make my own story more interesting: Isn't it cool that I have this funky alternative mom and didn't have to deal with all the "Is it wrong to question my sexuality?" stuff? I do have one friend who I haven't told, and I kick myself when I think about it, because once he gave me the perfect opportunity. I'm afraid another "right" time will never happen.

This right time was during a Thanksgiving I spent with my friend E. and his family. I'd met his mother and brother several months previously, and since we were well acquainted, the four of us were able to take refuge together from the rest of the family. We were talking about relationships, and they asked about my parents' divorce and whether either of my parents had remarried. I said that my dad had remarried and that my mom had been in a relationship for fourteen years. I did not mention that it was with a woman, which would have fit into the conversation, because we had been talking about other gay relationships and they'd said nothing negative about that option. They assumed, of course, because I steered them toward it, that I meant my mother was with a man. "Did you feel that he was your 'parent?'" they asked. "Absolutely," was my reply, and I said no more. I felt like such a traitor. I'd not told other people in the past and had felt bad about it afterwards, but I had never lied to a significant friend. I vowed that if anyone ever again asked me, I would just tell them. But it rarely seems to work that way or to be so straightforward.

How do you know when the time is right? As I said, I tend to use it in a "Gee, aren't I interesting" way, and when I'm getting to know someone, I look for openings in our conversations. There is often a point that feels right, when you've gone beyond superficial acquaintance toward trust and friendship. In the situation with E. and his family, part of me must not have been at ease. I'd already not told him for the year we'd known each other, and it would have been odd for me to tell him like that, with his family there. That was my way of rationalizing the feeling I had of betraying my mom and her partner. I still feel bad for not telling, and I still haven't told him.

As a kid, you learn to trust your instincts about who to tell and who not to tell. There were always two types of people in my world, those who knew and those who didn't. For the most part, people I'm attracted to as friends are people who I assume will be interested and supportive of my experience growing up. I tend to be comfortable around gay women and men and can usually manage to work the story of my life with many mothers into a conversation, which gives me immediate credibility. Now, I enjoy telling different kinds of people to see their reaction. And I always like it when people are curious and ask questions. "How did your mom tell you? Was that why your parents got divorced? Do you think it has affected you and your brother?" An ex-boyfriend told his parents about my mom. He told me that they were blasé about the information, and not particularly curious or intrigued. They said, "Well, it doesn't seem to have affected Lise." Left to tell them myself, I probably never would have, not expecting conservative, suburban parents to be supportive.

It's funny to think about my brother living with secrecy all the time. With his friends he can talk about mom being a therapist and growing up having to process everything in the path, but he can't really talk about growing up primarily among women. He also recently told me that most of his female friends are very independent, assured, and thoughtful, while many of his male friends tend toward the sexist and inconsiderate. I'm not sure why I think that's significant, but it seems related. He realized at some point in college that he was attractive to women, and boy, did he run with that. He is handsome and socially adept, but there's something else to him that most men lack.

He knows how to talk with women on a level that men don't often seem comfortable entering into. He knows how to look someone in the eye and say, "Tell me what's going on for you, and how can I be helpful?" He can find that inexplicable place where men and women can rarely communicate and talk about things, but he doesn't much like to talk about what is going on for him. He told me that when he's in a relationship, he can be expressive and straightforward, but when someone starts asking him to share his feelings, he backs up and away, distancing himself from the person who dares make him confront the murky stuff that is connected with mom.

I want him to feel comfortable telling people, not so much just to tell, but because for me, telling signifies understanding myself and being comfortable with the different-ness. I accept that my mother's difference is not mine, and that the power of choosing to tell need not restrict me and my relationships. I want him to understand these things now, but I must allow it to be on his time.

A Good
Example

Randi Levy

I'm eighteen and a college sophomore. I live at home with my mom and her lover in New York. I love to work with children and plan to center my career around them.

Linda Levy is a teacher, a lesbian, a public speaker, a listener, a leader, a lover, a daughter, and a mother. My mother. Many teenagers refuse to admit it, but I am clear that my mother has vitally affected my thinking and way of being in life.

Some teachers go to school, punch in, teach from a textbook for six hours and twenty minutes, punch out and go home. Not my mother. She is always trying new things and looking for fresh ideas. She is teaching the first and only coeducational folk dance class in New York City, and in addition, rather than teaching "textbook" health, she searches for contemporary readings that her students can relate to.

As a lesbian educator, my mother is a risk taker. Each time she comes out in a new school, she risks losing the friendship and trust of some uneducated students and colleagues. She must also sometimes face objections from scared and uninformed parents. The first time she came out, my mother attended a Parents' Association meeting in order to educate and reassure the parents about issues of homosexuality. Watching my mother take such care and interest in her work is very enriching. She has shown me that there is more to life than doing the expected minimum. When she comes home from school excited about a student who has grasped a concept she has presented, it makes me want to be able to give to someone and feel that same joy.

Growing up with my mother's openness about her lesbian lifestyle has encouraged me to become an open, honest, and broad-minded person. My mother has always been able to speak openly to people about her lesbianism, whether in the classroom, on a one-to-one basis, on television or radio, or in a workshop on homophobia. She realizes that she may not always get a positive reaction, but that doesn't matter to her. She knows that she is a good person and that what people think of her is irrelevant. In situations where my feelings have differed from others, I have sometimes worried that people will not like me if I tell them what my feelings are; then I recall how my mother has dealt with these instances. I remember that it doesn't matter how people feel about me as long as I feel good about myself. From my mother's positive example I know that in order to be true to myself, I must be open in the world.

From observing my mother's experiences with prejudice because of her lifestyle, I have learned that prejudice and stereotypes are useless in life. They only serve to hurt people and are never based on truth. I know that my mother is a perfectly normal human being; so are her lover and all of her lesbian and gay friends. I think that the same thing is true of people of all lifestyles, races, and creeds. Exposure to my mother's "different" lifestyle allows me to be more accepting of others.

A speaker, a listener, and a leader have all been my mother's roles in public forums as well as in the classroom. For over ten years, she has been a very active and involved member of a group called the New York City Gay Teachers Association. She represents this group at speaking engagements and workshops throughout the city. As the leader for the steering committee, she is responsible for selecting guest speakers, planning meetings and writing articles for the United Federation of Teachers newspaper. Our telephone number is printed as an information number for the association, so constant phone calls come in from around the county; some just for general questions, but many times a teacher is having a crisis and needs advice. My mother listens, reassures, gives information and support. My mother's pleasure in helping the people in her community is something I have always admired; because of this, I have recently joined a peer counseling group in order to help others in my community.

My mother's ability to show love and to accept love are the two things that have most helped me to be become a loving person. I have seen her as a lover, a daughter, and a mother. In all of these roles she has shown, and continues to show, warmth, support, affection, empathy, consideration, and care. My mother has always been there to guide me through rough times. The most important message my mother has conveyed to me throughout the years is that no matter what I do or say, she will always love me. Sometimes I go to her for advice, sometimes to find a listener, sometimes for reassurance . . . and sometimes just for a hug.

If There Were Only Mothers

Bob

I am ten years old and I live in Tallahassee, Florida. I have eight cats and am in the fifth grade. Most kids don't like school, but I'm different. I like it and I'm very good at math. I live with my mother and her friend Cindy.

My mother is different from other mothers, even though she is divorced. There are many mothers who are divorced, but my mother is a lesbian. I sometimes wonder how it would be if my parents stayed married. I don't know if there is any difference between people who are gay and other people, except for their private feelings. I have a lot of friends who are lesbians.

Some people think you need a father or a man around to help with the tough stuff, like the lawn and other things like that. I think it depends on what kind of job needs doing. I think anybody can do anything they want. Even if there were only mothers in the world, I think things would get done anyway. In fact, we just painted the house, my mom and Cindy and me.

My parents got divorced when I was still a baby. I have a brother who is twelve; he lives now with my father and my stepmother. I visit with him every other Easter, every other Christmas, and every summer. I don't get along with my brother very well. We're very different. He's lazy and doesn't like to play outside or get any exercise.

When I visit my dad he always says that it's wrong for my mom to be a lesbian. Both he and my stepmother say stuff about it every time I see them. He really doesn't like it. He says it's very wrong. He says he hates Cindy and that he doesn't like my mother very much. I don't like what either of them say, and it makes me feel pretty bad to hear it.

A couple times I told my father that my mother is not bad and that being a lesbian is not wrong. He still says it's wrong. That makes me angry, and then he gets angry. It's a little scary. He always brings it up and he always tells me that Cindy has no legal rights. He says that a lot.

Now that my brother is living with my dad, he thinks it's bad to be a lesbian, too. He's been listening to my dad. He used to think my mom was okay. My dad bribed him to live with him by offering a bigger allowance and more freedom.

I always thought that a normal family would have no problems. It seems impossible to have a normal family. But now I think everybody has problems.

No one at school knows about my mom. I think my friends would feel pretty bad if they knew. They would probably think it was wrong, too. And maybe they would feel sorry for me. I've thought about telling them, but I just never got around to it. I once had a friend spend the night and he had a good time, but I don't think he knew anything. I think the kids that don't like me would send rumors around the school.

I've lived with my mother's lover for over seven years. Most of the time we get along. She loves me a lot. Sometimes when I ask my mom something private, my mom's lover wants to know what it is, and I don't want her to know. She butts in sometimes.

I went to the Southern Music Festival with my mom. I liked the festival, except last time we couldn't go to the waterfall because it was closed. I see a lot of naked women there and I don't mind. The food is pretty good, but not great. The child care workers are really neat, especially Sandy.

Also at the festival I got my hair dyed by Lucie Blue Tremblay. Of course she colored it blue! I like to have my hair different ways, and once I had a mohawk. For a while I had a tail, and now I have stripes. The stripes are right by my ears, and the other day the fourth grade teacher asked me if I was wearing my glasses too tight!

Common Dumb Questions

Kirsten Chrust

I'm nineteen and presently in college in Wisconsin. I'm originally from Indianapolis.

I'm five feet seven inches, and weigh an occasional ten pounds more than I'd like. I have brown hair and hazel eyes. Sound pretty normal, eh? But there is something, for some reason, that sets me apart from a lot of people: my mother is a lesbian.

I don't really remember the first time my mother told me she was a lesbian. My parents were liberal, and I was raised to think of homosexuality as nothing more than another option. After dad died, when I was nine, I felt fine when she told me she was gay. I certainly wasn't ready for another daddy, and for some reason, because my mom's new lover was a woman, that made it all right. I thought I had it made. I guess I just didn't expect to confront some of the things that go along with having a lesbian mother.

Growing up is a hard enough thing to do, and I sometimes resented my mother for making it harder. I was a normal, insecure, developing pre-teen. I never really liked having the name Kirsten. It was always mispronounced, and I could never find anything with my name on it. (This problem gets easier the older I get: I don't really need monogrammed hair barrettes anymore!) Kirsten also rhymed with "Queer-stin," a nickname my creative peers stuck me with until high school rolled around. I couldn't understand why what my mother did behind closed doors mattered to other people, when what my "friends'" mothers did behind closed doors didn't matter. I enjoyed watching movies, making prank calls and eating pizza. I still liked boys. But none of what I did mattered, because of what my mother "had become." I was no longer considered normal because of the choices my mother had made.

After a while, the pain of other people's prejudices and rejections numbed, or maybe I got to the point where it didn't matter as much. But stupid feelings don't just vanish, and just as the kids in grade school rejected me as their friend, once I got into high school, boys thought my mother was reason enough not to date me. I would date a boy, and sooner or later I'd have to spring him with news of my family's hidden—or sometimes not so hidden—secret. Then there was his reaction. How silly it was that my mother's sexuality became a test of whether or not a relationship would last. Now I look back and know I wouldn't have wanted anybody that couldn't accept her anyway.

Now I've gone and made it sound like having a lesbian mother is the worst torture in the world. But believe it or not, I really think there are advantages to having a lesbian mother. I don't need to get embarrassed when I ask my mom's honey to pick me up some "feminine hygiene" products. Mom did, at one point, like men, and relationships are relationships because people are people, so she still understands about boyfriend problems.

I also experienced women's music festivals: vegetarian-munching, music-playing, hacky-sacking, and art-creating celebrations. Having a lesbian mother isn't a prerequisite for attending these festivals. In fact, my mother, my sisters and I attended these merrymakings before mom had her sexual metamorphosis. At the festival the weather was hot and humid, the roads were dusty dirt, and the accommodations were bring-your-own and carry-it-until-you-think-you-are-going-to-die. But looking back, the festivals were great. I'd sometimes bring my best friend and we'd pretend to "be together" to avoid being hit on. We'd barter back rubs for arts and crafts. And there was always the music, lying under the stars. Women's music stands out. Holly Near, Odetta, Sweet Honey in the Rock. Every one is worth listening to because the lyrics have something important to say. Women's festivals have helped me define what kind of music I will choose to listen to for the rest of my life.

Probably one of the most eye-opening experiences I've ever had took place when my mother, her lover and I had just come from a festival. I was fifteen. I had straight, scraggly hair and would have had to stuff a AA bra. We were dirty, smelly and hungry and in the middle of "This is my brother Darryl and this is my other brother Darryl" country. We stopped at a clean but creepy family restaurant. As we entered, I knew this was not anything like the ambience we had just left.

Willy Nelson's greatest hits played in the background, and the other customers were the kind of hairy, beer-bellied truck drivers who knew the waitress in the pink polyester uniform by her first and middle names. It was the kind of place that probably had National Rifle Association meetings in the back room. My mother and I were standing by the salad bar, admiring the veggies and feeling happy together. We told each other we loved one another, and we shared one of those mother-daughter peck kisses. Well, the next thing I knew, the pink polyester creature came and informed us that they wouldn't have "our kind" in their establishment. The rude woman had thought that my mother and I were lovers, and I don't think I've ever felt as ashamed as I did at that moment. My mother tried to explain that I was her daughter, but the damage had been done, and we left.

It wasn't like this memory scarred me for life; it was just that a mother and daughter kiss is something sacred to be treasured, something to remember on your first day away from home at college, or when you just wish mom was there to tuck you in. That incident made me realize some of the things that I take for granted, like going for walks and holding hands with my boyfriends, or hugging and kissing in public. If I were a lesbian, people would always be staring.

Most of the people in my life aren't homophobic, but I still don't think they'd be comfortable watching a homosexual kiss. It's a kind of denial: as long as homosexuals keep it to themselves, it's okay. It's unfair, but society sets it up this way. It seems to me that the only place homosexuals have to be comfortable expressing themselves are in places specifically designed for them. And the thought of keeping inside all the love you have for someone to be let out only behind closed doors makes me angry.

I thought I would end with some of the most common dumb questions I've been asked over the years, and some of the ways I've answered them:

If your mother's a lesbian, how can she have had children?
She learned from her mistakes.

If lesbians don't like men, why do they use "toys" that represent men's anatomy?
I guess they don't think every part of a man is bad.

What did your mom do with your dad after she decided she was queer?
She banished him to the "My wife's a dyke and I'm all alone" cult in New Jersey.

Does this mean you are a lesbian, too?
Yes; just ask my boyfriends!

Is that woman over there a lesbian?
I don't know; my mother never went to bed with her.

What do lesbians do in the bedroom?
I'm sure you'll find all the answers you need and more in *The Joy of Lesbian Sex*.

So you see, being the daughter of a lesbian seems at times to make people think I'm a doctor, therapist, librarian or even a psychic, when really all I am is a normal nineteen-year-old kid.

To wrap it all up, I would say being the daughter of a lesbian is the same and it's different. I don't always like the women my mother chooses to see, and sometimes I'm really happy with her decisions (like now). I'm sure the same would have been true if she stayed straight: I would have liked some men and hated others. Sometimes being her kid, it's hard for me to remember that her happiness is the most important thing in her life. So, although at some points along the way her being a lesbian made it a little hard or uncomfortable for me, it ultimately was worth it. I love my mom and she's happy.

Two Are
Better
Than One

Sara B.

*I'm six, almost seven. I
live with my mother and
my co-parent, Meg.
We've lived together for
two years. I have a
pet iguana.*

I have two mothers and other kids don't. I feel different. I don't tell most of my friends I have two mothers, but the ones that know think it's nice. I don't tell other kids at school about my mothers because I think they would be jealous of me. Two mothers is better than one. Nicole is my best friend, and she saw both my mothers because they came to pick me up. She asked if Meg was my big sister. I told her she was my co-parent, and she didn't know what that was. I told her it was like another mother, not my real mother. She was jealous.

When I was really little, I lived with my grandfather and grandmother because my mother was doing drugs. I got back with my mother when I was three. Then when I was four, my mother lived in this special house because she was getting off drugs. I stayed with my grandfather and grandmother again and I visited my mom every weekend. I was really glad she was off drugs. Then when I was five, we started to live together again. Sometimes I think it would be nice for all of us to live together, my grandma and grandpa and Meg and my mom and me. But there's a problem—my grandparents are going to buy a camper and travel around the world!

The first morning I found out that Meg was going to live with us was when I realized my mother wasn't sleeping in the loft with me. I cried, and then Meg came out and asked me what was the matter. I said, "Why are you here?" And then when my mother woke up I asked her why wasn't she sleeping with me, and I got mad at her for the whole day. Then Meg started to live with us. I was jealous of Meg for a while because she was so close to my mother. I don't feel differently about my mother and Meg, but Meg likes to wear dresses and my mother doesn't. I think of them both as my mother.

I feel kind of good and kind of bad about not having a dad. I don't have to listen to lots of orders from any dad, and I know my real dad was always drunk. I had another dad for a while, and he hit me all the time. I don't care if I have a mother and a father or a mother and a co-mother; I just want there to be two people. It's more fun with two.

Meg is going to have a baby next year, and I'll get to be a big sister. I'm going to be able to play with the baby while they give it attention so I won't be jealous. I know I'm going to be jealous, but I'm happy, too, and sometimes mad. I know I'm not going to get as much attention as I do now. I hope they have a girl, because I would like to dress her up really nice. Also I want to give my Barbies to the little one, so I hope it's a sister.

My mother was adopted and so she has two sets of parents. I haven't met her real parents, but they are dying to meet me. I see her other parents a lot. They spoil me, and they like Meg and all of us.

I have thousands of friends that are lesbians. I mostly see them at AA meetings and they all say "Hi" to me.

They're real nice. I also have some friends who are men who are together with other men. Dick and Dave are these men who are giving us sperm. We're putting it in a bag and using a little shooter thing. They're going to be the dads of our baby.

Last year my teacher found out. She saw both of my moms at PTA night, and she talked to both of them about me. I didn't want her to know, because I wanted her to think I had a mother and a father. I don't know why. I guess because I wanted her to think of me the same as the other children. They might think of me differently, but I don't really know what they'd think. This year I wanted my real mother to go to PTA night and Meg to stay home with me. Then next year Meg could go to PTA night and my real mother could stay home with me. We're moving soon; we're going to live close to Dick and Dave. I want to send my address to the teacher so we can be pen pals like we are with the kids in Japan.

My moms are very good moms. They don't bug me, they don't swear at me, they don't hurt me. They don't order me around. They play with me, and they talk to me about the things that are going on in my life. Like if boys are chasing you and you don't want them to, like some boys were today. I told Meg and Ma about it, and they talked to me about it and thanked me for telling them. If someone asked me if I was a happy kid, I'd say yes, yes, yes, yes!

Out of the
Pain

Michael

I'm a twenty-seven-year-old man. I don't identify with any racial grouping, nor do I like people to identify my racial identity for me. My mother is Japanese-American. My father was Irish. I have seven years of college experience, including a B.A. in Classical Liberal Arts. I'm a technical writer for a firm which serves nuclear and intelligence companies.

L esbians should not fill their children with their own fears and hatreds. I say this after considering the causes of needless pain in my past, and my troubles understanding the present.

I was eleven when my mother sat me down and told me she was a lesbian. It meant nothing to me. I was living with her, but I didn't understand what she was saying. She kept her sex life out of the small one-bedroom apartment we lived in.

Her confession came a few years after her divorce, at which time she left me with my disciplinary stepfather. He was the sort of clean-cut, honest, working man who abused me sexually, physically, and emotionally.

My mother came to school one day and took me away from him (I didn't know why), and I found myself on the other coast of the country. Today they would call this parental kidnaping. I now suspect she knew her action was illegal, so telling me about her lesbianism was, in part, a preparation for anything my stepfather might try in retaliation.

I was very troubled at that time; reclusive, quiet, withdrawn, unsocial. I was sent to private psychiatric therapy and, at the recommendation of my shrink, did group therapy for a long time. But I refused to communicate with the therapists. I didn't want to talk about what had happened, and, in retrospect, I don't think I understood what had happened. I think I was in a sort of shock or trauma. Also, the fact that the shrinks were male probably didn't help. From about the time of the divorce on (I was seven or eight), I was the kid whom all other kids—including the kids who got picked on—picked on.

Throughout the next few years (ten to sixteen) I met lesbian friends of my mother's who also had kids. I think our meeting was a deliberate act on her part for me to meet other kids of lesbians, perhaps so we would feel we weren't alone as children of gay parents. I can't recall any conversations about the sexual orientation of our mothers. I don't think we really understood or cared about it. But I do recall our wishing our mothers were more attentive to us than to each other. We kids would get together and have sex, males or females in any combination—unbeknownst to our parents, but ironically I don't think any of us really knew what our mothers' lesbianism really meant.

Sometime in sixth grade I joined the Boy Scouts, and it was then that I started to be called a new word: faggot. It took quite a long time before I understood what that new word meant. I think that one word was really harmful to my development, because it pointed to the stigma about not being heterosexual. Since my parents had sex with the same sex (my mother with other women, my stepfather with me), I had not understood that homosexuality was wrong. Also, at the time I couldn't figure out my own sexuality, because I was having sex with people of both sexes. This is all in retrospect, because all I understood at the time was that there was this word—faggot—and associated with that word was the feeling that people didn't like me. The word itself didn't have meaning, but together with the intent I could tell it was a bad thing to be.

The other most signicant event of that time in the early seventies was that my mother was involved in the radical feminist lesbian movement in Washington, D.C. She would take me to various meetings in dark underground places. I was being exposed to damaging experiences. What she didn't really know was that we kids—and I was twelve at the time—would be left with other lesbians who said horrible things to us. I distinctly remember a woman telling me, "You are a most despicable thing on earth because you are nothing but a future man." I understand now that there was a lot of hatred in the entire country at that time, and that women were just starting to voice their rage, but for me, this kind of hatred ruined my life.

This hatred, of men by women, of women by myself, has existed in my life until recently, because I could not relate to women with trust. I could not believe that women had any healthy, honest emotional or sexual desire for me. Firstly, because I was picked on by my schoolmates; and secondly, because these adult women told me these horrible things. Not all lesbians were awful to me, but there were enough abusive ones to beat down my already low self-esteem. The strange thing is that my mother never had anything to do with any of this herself. It was a by-product of her lesbianism. The lesbians who did not have children were the ones who screwed everything up. There was a stigma among them about having kids. There was no adult around whom I could share this with. (Perhaps a man, not an abuser, could have listened and helped me put it in perspective. Someone like myself now, whom I could have talked to. He could have just said, "Some women are lousy mothers.")

Until I was sixteen or so, I was sexually abused by many straight men, "friends" of my mother's whom I was occasionally left with. I wondered, what was going on on this planet? The end result of all of this abuse is that today I don't trust people. Period. On the other hand, I don't have anything to hide from anyone, because I know I have done nothing wrong. Other people have done things which were wrong. I abused others myself when I was a youth, but once I became aware of the pattern—I was abused and therefore I abused—I stopped.

When I was thirteen, I had a major accident at school and we moved to California. I was really bent out of shape. I had lost one eye. There was a great deal of trauma and pain with that loss, and, in addition, I suddenly hit puberty. I was forced by circumstance to learn to take care of myself. My mother was involved in her own life. From that point on she was very neglectful. In simple words—she was a lousy mother. Her friends thought so, too.

When I was fourteen she took a lover whom she has been with ever since. This lady and I now have a quiet truce, but it was hard for me when they got together, because their relationship started in the middle of my adolescence. Our fights had little to do with lesbianism and a lot to do with someone coming in and taking away what little attention I was getting.

With the lack of supervision and so on, I was into drugs by the age of fifteen. My life went downhill for the next several years. It was the late seventies, I was in Berkeley, on drugs, and I tried everything. I got in some trouble, but nothing serious—fortunately. I was somehow smart enough, even on drugs, not to get totally immersed in trouble.

I hit rock bottom at nineteen. I didn't like where I was at, and I decided to change. I had barely graduated from high school with a D- average, but I managed to persuade St. John's College, one of the best liberal arts colleges in the United States, to accept me. I worked before and during college to save money and pay my way, and I got my degree.

At college I was accepted for what I was, what I felt, and what I understood. I found things that made my life worth living. The college is a very close-knit community, and I found my own family.

Since I turned seventeen my relationships have all been heterosexual, except for a couple of one-night stands with men in the pre-AIDS era. With AIDS now, I'm not about to go back into that community. But I am very tolerant of all persuasions of thought or belief. I enjoy talking with people who think and believe differently than I do, because the world has room for all of us, regardless of our opinions. I don't like radicals personally, but they have a place as well as I do. When someone has strong opinions about a cause, I turn off. I don't fight for any cause, because I know better than to be deceived by promoters of causes. I believe that people in causes are motivated by selfishness, not by principle. I learned this by experiencing the various abuses people in causes laid upon me.

Over the last few years it's been up and down with my mother. We got close several years ago and now our communication is very poor—again, none of this has anything to do with her being a lesbian. I've discovered that if I'm fifteen hundred miles away we get along great, but if we're within thirty miles, forget it. Since I've moved back from college, she has turned our relationship into monetary exchange. We don't communicate much about anything else. I attribute this to her becoming a lawyer while I was gone.

My mother seems very closeted and socially fearful right now. There's a lot of gay paranoia in the country, so she may be justified in her feelings. She used to be out of the closet. Now she seems worried about being found out. It's her decision, and she lives whatever way she wants to. But I am telling this story because this is my experience and I have nothing to hide.

Though my mother was a lesbian, her lesbianism had nothing to do with how she raised me. She wasn't there for me when I needed discipline or parental support. She was out with the girls instead of being at home when her child needed her. This was no different than my friends whose straight, married parents were out doing their thing. This is the reason why lesbianism is the excuse for some of the stuff that happened, but not the cause. She was busy being a lesbian when she could have been a parent.

Critics might say, "Hey, you turned out all right." I agree. But I was blessed with enough innate intelligence and fortitude to figure out how to look after myself. I don't know how other kids of lesbians ten to twenty years ago turned out. I know many of us were unhappy at that time.

Anywhere there is hatred, it gets taken out on children. Lesbians who hate or fear men take this out on boy children. I suspect that same thing might happen with gay fathers and girl children. I know there are a great many more children in heterosexual families who are far more screwed up than children of gay parents because there is more sexual abuse in these families. I don't like to see abuse of kids in any society.

People filled with hatred in turn filled me with hatred. Only through my strength of character, over the last few years, have I been able to overcome the hatred and see my true self. I still avoid people and have trouble being close to people, but this, too, will pass. I've been trying to make women happy. It's taken me to the past year to understand that I have to be myself; other people have to make themselves happy. A few female lovers have described me as emotionally withdrawn, difficult to talk with, at times not there, exclusive, shut in. I find relationships hard to believe in. For the most part, I can't understand why people have them. I don't know what a normal relationship is supposed to be like. I have no example of how to behave, feel, express feelings, or sympathize with another's feelings. This annoys my lovers to no end, since I don't pay attention when I should and am obnoxiously attentive when they'd rather be left alone. I have a lot of experiences; I just don't feel them very deeply. I have built such immense and thick walls around my spirit that nothing but the thinnest vein of emotion seeps through.

I retain tight behavioral control at the expense of a rich emotional life in order to survive. I dream of a world where this never happened. I have survived by staying in shallow water.

A Problem
Partner

Jessica

I'm nineteen and I work at a day care center. I'm in college and planning to be a social worker. I live in a large city in the Midwest. For the past seven or eight years I've lived with my mother and her lover. My mother and dad have been divorced since before I was two.

The day my mother's lover was going to move in, my mother told me about their relationship. I was ten years old, and before that I had no idea what was going on. I didn't think about it much. I just said yeah, okay. At the time I didn't really know what it meant.

My mother has her doctorate and she works at a large university. From what I understand, my mother met her lover at college; I think my mother was her teacher. Five years later they got together, and they've been together now nine years.

I have never gotten along with my mom's lover. She's a nurse, and when I was growing up she wasn't often home when I was, and even at this point, our lives sometimes never cross. But she's real stubborn and has a problem with drinking. When she got together with my mom, she had never really been around other children; I was the first one. I was just being me, being a kid, but I thought she was really aggressive, and she scared me. She still scares me, but she really scared me then. She's really quiet except when she drinks. Then, if she's happy, she'll talk to me about school and be a friend to me, but if I do something she feels is wrong, she'll get really angry. She says things she wouldn't normally say. When she's drinking she doesn't really have a middle ground; she is either angry or happy.

In high school things were both good and bad. I don't know; maybe things would have been the same with any stepparent. If I got my way, I liked her. If I didn't, I didn't like her. But I think it's slightly different than a second marriage sort of thing, or having a stepfather. I might have been hostile if my mother was with a man, but I wouldn't have had to deal with the gay issue. The problems would have been different.

My mom didn't want to get in the middle of the fighting. She would tell me to talk to her lover, and that's something I could never really do. It was too hard. When things were okay I didn't want to disturb the calm waters, and when things were bad it was just too difficult to talk.

This was hard for my mother; I didn't want to make her unhappy, but didn't know what else to do. My mom and I went to counseling for a while to figure this out, and sometimes her lover came also, but then she stopped.

Throughout the years I've seen a lot of counselors, but now I'm seeing someone who is helping me to understand a lot what happened when I was younger. She has helped me to realize that the situation at home wasn't my fault, that I was feeling similar to other kids who had gay parents. I learned that even if I couldn't talk things out with my mother's lover, that I could work things out for myself.

There was a time when I was angry at my mom because I thought her being gay wasn't fair to me. I didn't understand it, and I thought she'd get over it. There were times I wanted to make her lover so mad that she would leave, and there were times she was going to leave. Then I'd talk to my mother and feel really bad, because she really loved her and wanted her to stay. I wanted my mother to be happy, and for the most part she seemed happy. But sometimes it looked to me like she'd do anything her lover said to do. It was almost like she'd try anything to please her, like a puppy dog. I hated to see that, and I'd get mad at both of them and the whole situation. That's changed now, for the better.

I've never found my mother's being gay to be a problem with my friends, although I haven't told a lot of people about it. Sometimes I felt embarrassed about her, but I always knew it wasn't my fault. My closest friends wouldn't say anything about it unless I wanted to talk. I did need to talk sometimes, and my mother said I could talk to her, but I couldn't talk to her about her lover. So it helped that my friends accepted.

My grandmother has dealt with my mother being gay the best she can. She doesn't like it, and she was worried about me living with lesbians. She is so prejudiced against everyone—blacks, gays, and anyone who is not like her—that I never told her much because I knew she'd get the wrong idea. She always tries to get my mother to feel guilty about her life, and I don't want that to happen.

My mother has also worried about my dad finding out about her being gay, in case he wanted to get me back. I never thought that was a big deal, because he never really wanted me, even before she was gay. Once when things were bad I asked to live with him, but he said only if my mother paid him child support. He hadn't paid for me when I was younger, so this didn't seem right. Apparently he suspected my mother was gay, but didn't know if I knew. My mother maintained that he didn't know, and for a while everyone pretended nothing was going on. He has been married four times and blames women for everything. He says his marriage to my mom didn't work because of her being gay, but my mother says she didn't know she was gay until a long time after the divorce. I believe my mother more than I do my dad; he sometimes bends the truth to make it into what suits him best.

Sometimes I wondered if I was going to turn out to be gay, and that scared me. I didn't know if you could catch being gay. I asked my counselor about this and was told it wasn't true. In the back of my mind I sometimes still worry about this. I think kids of lesbians need to know that you don't end up being gay because your parents are—unless you want to. Also, kids need to accept their parents and get on with their own life; it doesn't help to keep agonizing about someone else's life. You need to deal with things and then move on.

I'm engaged to be married now, and my fiancé likes my mother and doesn't mind her being gay. My mother is very cheerful, outgoing, and funny, and he gets along well with her. Sometimes he has differences with her lover, but then everyone seems to. Both of them have helped him out a lot, financially and otherwise. He's German and his family is in Germany. They don't know anything about my family, but they are nice people and I don't think they'll mind when they find out. We're planning a long engagement, so that may be a long way off.

My mother has many friends who are gay, many of whom are men. I like all of them very much. Until recently I didn't know there were so many resources available to gays and lesbians. I didn't know there were newspapers and bookstores and all that. I never imagined that people so condemned by society would have their own newspapers and be so open about what they do. I thought people just found each other by word of mouth. I was suprised everything was so open. It's obvious to me that my mother is gay; you can tell by the way she talks about her life, her lover, her friends. But there are so many people who don't want to know about gay people that they just don't see it. I have never really met anyone who was totally against gay people, but I know they must be out there, because otherwise it wouldn't be such a big deal.

I really am proud of my mom. She's a wonderful person. Aside from the situation with her lover, I really have no problems with her being gay. Maybe if I had met her lover on the street, we could have been friends. But growing up with her was hard, and sometimes it still is.

Like Sisters

Zea and Aarin

Zea: I'm thirteen years old. I live in San Francisco with my mom. Sometimes I stay with my mom's ex-lover. Aarin is like my sister because I am really close to her mother, Nan. My whole name is Zea Nachama Eugenia Mabwa. My mother is black and my father is Greek.

Aarin: I'm six and have two moms. One is Nan and one is Lisa. They live in separate houses. I stay with both of them, switching off.

Aarin: I found out that my mom is a lesbian the first time I went to a gay and lesbian parade. I was about four. I knew that being a lesbian was being a woman who got together with another woman.

Zea: I found out about my mom on my own somehow.

When I was about five someone explained to me about sex, and then I figured that there were people who got together with their own sex.

Aarin: I have a dad, but I haven't known him all my life. My moms are trying to find where he is, because I really want to know him. Other kids don't believe that I have a dad, and I do—I just don't know who he is. Sometimes they tease me about it because all of them have dads. It makes me feel bad; it hurts my feelings. They understand that I have two moms, but they don't really believe that either. They think that one of my moms is a fake mom. They don't understand about people not having a mom and a dad. I'm different than all the other kids in my class.

Zea: Through preschool no one really saw that my family was different, but when I was in third grade we were doing something for Father's Day. I told people I didn't have a dad, and they started laughing because they thought it was a joke. They weren't laughing to be mean, but they couldn't believe I didn't have a dad. In fifth grade I brought in a picture of my mothers for Mother's Day and they didn't tease me any longer.

I don't like when kids make fun of you. I know how that is. Sometimes white kids make fun of my hair—they call me "poodle." They aren't racist out in the open, but there are only three black kids out of sixty-five kids in my grade. I'm sick of it. But none of those kids know about my mothers. Sometimes they call other people "homos" or "fags" and I will ask them why they say that kind of stuff. But I've never told anybody about my moms. If it did get around, I think I would be treated differently because of my mom's sexuality.

I think that even if my mom wasn't a lesbian, I wouldn't be prejudiced, but I would feel less comfortable around gay people. I might feel differently if I found out someone was a lesbian. Because of my mother I have a different viewpoint and perspective. I think I'm more open-minded than other kids. I have a lot of women in my life, a lot of "godmothers."

I don't have many men in my life, so I'm not as comfortable around them as I would like to be.

Aarin: I'm the only kid in my school with a lesbian mother, so I feel special and different. Sometimes I get called names like "No-Dadhead" and that makes me feel bad. Some boys are always looking for a way to make you cry. And I'm the only one in my whole school that doesn't have a dad.

Zea: Being different from other kids wouldn't be so bad if lesbians and gay men weren't looked down on.

There are very few kids with single parents in my school, and I know that if kids found out I'd be judged. I can't imagine what people would say. Maybe kids wouldn't want to come over to my house, or maybe their parents wouldn't let them come over. I think the older I get, the more pressure there is from other kids. When you are young, kids don't really understand, and they haven't been so influenced by society.

I wish sometimes that we had a dad that lived with us. I have never met my dad, but I do know who he is. I am interested in knowing more about him, and I ask my mom a lot, but we don't know how to find him. I feel a little uncomfortable asking my mom about it, because she feels uncomfortable talking about him. Sometimes I get different stories about him.

Aarin: Kids make fun of you for all different reasons. Since I don't have a dad, when it's Father's Day I always do something for my grandfather. I consider him my dad. I always sent him cards, but now he is dying, and soon I won't have anyone to send cards to. This makes me sad.

My friend's parents just got a divorce and she was really sad. Every day we walked out in the field and talked about it. I said, "I know it's hard. I know it's really confusing; every day you wonder what's going to happen. That's how it was when my moms split up, and now I feel better." Now this friend is feeling better about her problems because of what I said.

I know it's hard to live in two different houses. And sometimes I don't know what I'm doing on a certain day, or who is taking me to soccer practice. Now I have a schedule and I spend part of the week with each of my moms. Sometimes it's confusing. On Fridays Zea is with me and we have Shabbos dinner together with Nan.

I know a lot about AIDS because my mother works at a place where they talk to and work with people who have AIDS. I've met a lot of people with AIDS, men and women and children, too. A lot of times I help her with xeroxing and stuff at the place she works. Everyone there is very nice.

Last summer my mother and I delivered food to people with AIDS, people who were too weak to get their own food. Sometimes it was really hard because we met these people and then they wouldn't be on the route any longer because they had died.

Zea: I think it's really hard for kids of lesbians. One day people will change their views. Even if they think it's wrong, eventually everyone won't be so prejudiced against gays.

I don't know if I'm gay or straight, but I don't feel pressure to be either way. But when I was being born, I heard that my mom and Nan made a balloon out of a rubber glove that said, "Gay or Straight, That's Okay" on it.

I've liked most of the women that my mom has been in relationships with. This time I feel like her relationship is really inconvenient, because right now I need more attention than she is giving me. Sometimes I've told my mother about something I have to do on a certain night, and she'll make other arrangements for me because she will have forgotten or wasn't really listening to me. I think this would be true if she had a boyfriend, though.

I'm still close to most of the women who my mother has been with. I spend one weekend a month with one woman, and another one I see two times a week. Sometimes I wish there was a second person in the house so when my mom goes out there would be someone else to watch me. But it would be very hard to explain things to my friends if my mom and another woman shared a bed.

Aarin and I consider ourselves sisters because Nan is like one of my mothers. When Nan was pregnant with Aarin I got jealous, and then when she was young I got jealous at different times. But I have been around the whole time Aarin was growing up.

Aarin: Sometimes we fight like sisters, but every day I love Zea more and more and more.

———— • ————

Editor's Note: Soon after this interview, Aarin actually found out the identity of her father by way of a third party. He is a gay writer who lives on the East Coast. She met with him over Father's Day weekend. I asked her to talk about that incredible meeting.

Aarin: On the special night when I met Andy—that's my dad's name—he came and started hugging everybody. I thought, "This is strange," and I ran into my room. At first I thought I should act like somebody else, but I knew I should really be like myself. It was a little bit scary. I kept thinking he wasn't really the real thing. But it was such a special thing to be able to meet him.

The first and second meetings were funny because you find out about all these relatives. I met new family and they met me, and I was sometimes confused. I was sad when he left, because he lives far away.

I like my dad. He is very nice. Meeting him was worth waiting for. I kept asking to meet him, and my parents were trying to find him, but it took a long time. I hope other kids who meet their dads find they have nice dads. You never know what your dad is going to be like, but you can only hope he is very kind.

Sometimes I thought I would never meet my dad. My parents kept saying I might not meet him, but I didn't believe them. You have to believe you are going to meet him someday. I think it depends on what kind of person you are whether or not you really want to meet him or not. I *really* wanted to meet my dad.

Now I have two moms and one dad. One mom had me, and I really feel as though she is my mom. I call her mom. I call my other mom "Ima"—that means "mom" in Hebrew. Andy is like a father who cares and loves me, but he lives far away, and so he's not like a real parent. But he's handsome and nice and loving to me. I am going to go to family camp with him later this summer. We are going to fish and stay in cabins. I think maybe one of our grandmas is going, and maybe my two grandpas. Some aunts and cousins are going. And my moms are going, too!

It feels different now that I have met my dad. When I really look at him, I can see the match between us. There are things about myself that are like my dad. I even look a bit like him.

Making
Family

Guilemere

I am black, five years old, and in the first grade. I live in North Carolina with my mommy and my "Aunt Shari." Even though Aunt Shari is not my real mommy, I'm a lot like her. She's white, though.

I think my mommy is happy the way that she lives. Mommy told me that people are married in different ways—man to man, woman to woman, or man to woman. These are all relationships. She told me she likes her relationship and that she doesn't want to change her relationship.

I feel happy about that because I like having Aunt Shari living with us. I was four when my mommy met her, and they got married when I was five. I call her Aunt Shari because she and my mommy told me I could call her whatever I wanted. I asked her to be my fake aunt because she is already an aunt, a real one. And I wanted her as my aunt. And I like Aunt Shari's family; she has a sister who has kids and I like those kids.

My own family I don't like very much. I don't like

my grandma, because she didn't want my mom to marry Aunt Shari. My grandmother gets mad because my mom is going to marry someone who is white. I wonder, how come Uncle Tim can marry Paula, who is white, but my mom can't marry Shari?

My grandmother says bad things about Aunt Shari. She said she wanted to shoot her. One time my grandmother went to this person who helps other people hurt people that they don't like. She tried to put a spell on Aunt Shari, to hurt her. That hurt my mommy's feelings and it hurt mine, too. I wanted to go to the police so they would get my grandmother and stop her.

I don't want to grow up gay, because it's hard. There's a lot of argues and stuff. Like with my grandma and that spell she put on. And when I go visit her she says bad things about Aunt Shari, and about white people. She's too mean. If she doesn't like us, she shouldn't call and she shouldn't ask me to come over. Sometimes I just want to get away from her. One day she called and asked me out and I wanted to go. But then I thought about it and changed my mind. I'm tired of her face; sometimes I just want to smack her.

I know a lot of people who have dads. My best friend has a dad, and Aunt Shari has a dad that died already. I have friends that come over to play, but mostly they don't know that mommy and Aunt Shari are gay. I tell them Aunt Shari is our roommate. We don't have a very big house, so sometimes they ask things. When they ask her if she is married to a woman, she tells them it isn't their business.

I'm a lot like Aunt Shari. You know, whatever she eats, I eat. She likes hot dogs, I like hot dogs. We're junk food eaters, and my mommy only eats healthy food. One day me and Aunt Shari got stuck into trouble. Mommy left the house early in the morning, and when she did we snuck and ate all these goodies! We snuck into the cupcakes—for breakfast! Later mommy found the crumbs and the chocolate mess. She got mad, but we didn't want to eat breakfast—we wanted to have snackies!

I spend lots and lots of time with Aunt Shari, because my mom used to work at night. We do everything together. She plays with me and helps me with my feelings, and I'm happy to have two moms because it's different. One borned me in her stomach and the other helps me with my homework. Sometimes when they argue, it hurts my ears and I want to leave the house. When Shari told me she and my mom were getting a divorce I was scared and unhappy, but when she told me they were getting married again I was happy!

Some friends ask me questions about my moms, and I get embarrassed and scared to answer. And sometimes I'm mad that I don't have brothers and sisters. I really want more kids in our family. All I have is cousins, and they are boring. Once I told Aunt Shari and mommy to get married to men and have babies. Then they could tell the men to live in another state!

Your Mama!

Paul and Amanda

*"Paul" and "Amanda"
are foster kids who have
lived in San Francisco
with Sally and Irene
for the last five years.
Paul is now ten,
Amanda, nine. They
ran away from their
abusive home at the ages
of four and five. Sally
and Irene have been
involved in a long legal
process to assure
final adoption.*

Paul: When we met Sally we were on a trip to this amusement park with other foster kids. We talked with her a lot and sat next to her on the bus. We really liked her. That was five years ago.

Amanda: After that we met Irene. Once we went to a park together and they said we could stay there as long as we wanted, until we got tired. So we stayed there until midnight!

Paul: No, it wasn't midnight. It was only really late. A couple of months later we moved in with them. I didn't think then it was weird to have two moms, and I still don't. Sometimes I call them both mom, sometimes I call them by their names.

Amanda: When I'm mad I yell, Sally! When I'm not mad I call her mom.

Paul: It took a while to find out about Irene and Sally being together. When we started to spend the nights with them, we noticed that they stayed in the same room together.

But there's nothing different about having two moms. These moms are nice to have, because they are nicer to us than if we had a mom and a dad. We're lucky. I think it's funner to have two moms, and I think its fine for lesbians to adopt kids.

Amanda: Two ladies are better than a mom and a dad. I'm a girl. So now there's three of us against one of him! We win!

Paul: But I count the boy-cat, too.

Amanda: You know when other kids say "Your Mama"? It's a bad thing to say. But when they say it to me I say, "Which one?" Some kids think we have two dads, too! But we have two stepmoms and no dads.

Paul: They're not stepmoms, they're adoptive moms. If they were stepmoms they'd be married to our dad. Yuck!

My real mom wants us to live here. And most of my friends know about us having two moms and it's okay with them, too.

If I ever have kids, I'd want to adopt them. I'd like to help other kids who don't have families.

Not So Different

Keoki *I am thirteen years old and live in a small town in Hawaii with my mother. I live with my father on the weekends.*

My mother was a lesbian before I was born. My mom and dad were never married. They were together for a short while about two years after she came out. My dad has never said anything bad about my mother being gay. He has other children now. I told my stepbrother and sister about my mother, and they didn't seem to care.

I've been around gay people all my life. I like it when my mother has lovers, because she seems happier then. There was one lover my mother wasn't very happy with, but I liked her as a person anyway.

My mother is active in the lesbian community, and she edits a lesbian/gay newsletter. Some kids at school have teased me about my mother being gay, and this makes me mad. I think it's a stupid thing to tease someone about. They call all gay people "fags" and "lezzies." I'm sure that this happens everywhere, not just in Hawaii and not just with teenagers, but with everyone everywhere. Sometimes I tell people to shut up when they say that kind of stuff. I tell them that gay and lesbian people are no different than they are, except they're attracted to someone of their own sex. I don't think those kids have ever thought about what it would be like to be gay or lesbian and to have people make fun of you—or even beat you up.

Because of my mother's work, we've received crank calls saying all kinds of things that are prejudiced against gay and lesbian people. It's scary, and for this reason I sometimes wish my mother was straight.

And it's difficult to bring people to the house. There's stuff about lesbianism all over the house, lesbian books and things. I think this stuff would be a problem for my friends, so I don't bring them home much. I don't want to give them more opportunity to tease me. Right now my mother isn't so open about it because I've asked her not to be.

Some people think that if your mother is gay, you will be too. But that's stupid. If your mother has black hair it doesn't mean you will too. Or if your mother has a birthmark, you won't have one in the same place. Being gay is not something you inherit.

My mother is an unusual woman, not because she's a lesbian but just because she's different. People think lesbians are different somehow from other people, and they aren't. I think if kids got to know lesbians, and saw what kind of people they are, then they would be more understanding.

I'm Always Looking for My Mother

Carla Tomaso

I live in Southern California where I teach English at a girls' high school and write fiction and plays. Several of my plays have been produced locally, and my stories have been collected by Seal Press in the first edition of Voyages Out. *While my relationship with my mother has influenced all my work, I've never written about my experiences as directly as I have here.*

It was about two in the afternoon when I eagerly climbed the long flight of outdoor steps to my godmother's studio. I was supposed to meet my mother there after school. It was the late fifties. I was in the third grade, and I thought my godmother was pretty far-out. I liked going to Connie's place, for one thing because it was the messiest room in the world, full of books and canvases and dirty brushes. It smelled good too, like wood and oil paint. Best of all, though, Connie was nice to me. She treated me more like a friend than a kid. She'd been my mother's best friend forever; people sometimes thought they were sisters because they looked so much alike.

When I opened the door I saw everything at once. My mother was lying naked on the couch across the room, posing for Connie, who was standing at her canvas with her back to me, painting. For a moment everything froze. Then Connie laughed, my mother covered herself, and I walked further into the room. Nothing was wrong. Connie had been painting my mother, but everything seemed strange; my mother was explaining too much and Connie wasn't laughing anymore. We went home right away.

Another time, not long after, I walked into the studio and heard voices coming from the bathroom. The door was open partway and I saw my mother kneeling at the side of the bathtub, washing Connie's back. They were both laughing until they saw me. This time my mother seemed angry, as if I'd interrupted something important, something private, and I felt hurt and excluded. I went outside, breathing hard. Then I began to cry.

In my memories, I'm always looking for my mother and finding her with women doing things I don't understand. Sometimes the women aren't as nice as Connie, who even employed me as a flower girl in one of her weddings. Sometimes they blame me for opening a door that wasn't even locked.

It was summer vacation a year later when my mother brought me to a beach party given by some of her friends on the bowling team. I was the only child, and I soon got bored playing on the beach all by myself. Also, I had just noticed that my mother wasn't with the group of women sitting in the sand, drinking beer and talking. I started to get very panicky, but I remembered to act calm, because she wouldn't have liked it if I'd made a scene. Besides, I knew in my head that she wouldn't actually leave me. Finally, somebody pointed me up to the beach house to find her. The front door was wide open, but I couldn't see her anywhere. I began to get frantic. I called out to her but there wasn't any answer. Finally I noticed a door that I hadn't yet opened. Inside I saw a big bed. My mother sat up suddenly and stared at me. She was with Barb, a woman I didn't like, especially when she was drinking. And then Barb shouted, "You fucking sneaking brat!" at me as I stood in the doorway. My mother never said a word.

One day when I was eleven, my father moved out. I blamed my mother, even though she'd made sure I knew that he'd been having a messy affair with Judith, a divorcee from the country club. My mother told me a lot of bad things about my father, but I didn't take her seriously because I knew what she was like when she was upset. I also knew that she wanted him back, because she asked me what she should buy him as a present. She gave him a bicycle, but he still didn't return. He dutifully visited me on Sundays and told me he loved me. I knew that the reason he didn't ask about my mother was because he didn't love her.

My mother begged him to return, drank, had a minor car accident. A few months passed. One day when I came home from school, she introduced me to Nancy. I was wearing my pastel uniform with the embroidered H for Hillside, my prep school, on the pocket. School had become very important to me, and I could hardly wait to get to my room to start my homework, but I reluctantly put my books down on the coffee table to meet her. Nancy looked sort of strange for a friend of my mother's. As we shook hands, I decided she looked more like a skinny man than a woman, and I also decided that I didn't like her at all. For one thing, she didn't look at me when she talked, and for another, she was wearing tight jeans and cowboy boots. Before I went to my room, my mother told me that Nancy was going to stay with us for a while because she didn't have a place to live right then.

Nancy never moved out. In fact, when we bought a new house, Nancy had her own bedroom, a monastic, white rectangle with a twin bed and western novels stacked in the bookcase. She didn't seem to have many possessions or much of a life from before she met my mother through the bowling team. And it didn't take me long to realize that she wasn't sleeping in her own bedroom. She slept in my mother's room, on one of the twin beds united by a common headboard. I became obsessed by the design of this bed. Was it two twins or a single king? The bed took on an ambiguous symbolism that I struggled with and tried to repress for the four years that I lived with my mother and Nancy. I only caught them touching once: holding hands in front of the television news report announcing Kennedy's death. My mother pulled her hand away when I entered the room.

I came to hate Nancy with a fire-hot intensity. Telephone operators called her "sir." She was a conversational know-it-all but couldn't pronounce obvious words correctly. My mother seemed to support her financially. Nancy told my mother how to behave and told me what a bastard my father was for trying to cut off my mother's alimony payments. I learned later that every year he told the judge that my mother was in a lesbian marital relationship, and because it was as if she was married, he shouldn't be required to support her. The judge, every year, sliced a big chunk off the payment.

But mostly I came to hate Nancy because of the way she and my mother fought every night. They screamed and bickered and whined and pouted over everything. Nancy frequently got in her car and left the house late at night because she was so angry. Once, on a vacation in the desert, Nancy closed my mother's hand in the car door by mistake after a particularly nasty drunken scene in a restaurant. I found myself being almost certain that she did it on purpose. I tried to pity my mother as a helpless victim, but soon I came to hate her, too. She hadn't been particularly passive with my father; why should she have been now? And if she loved me, why did she put me through all this? Why didn't she just throw Nancy out?

My father remarried about a year after Nancy moved in, and once or twice I got so angry with my mother or Nancy that I ran away from home and spent the night at his house, which was conveniently nearby. Finally, my mother told me that she and Nancy were going to move to the beach. She came into my bedroom one evening and sat on my bed, and for a moment I felt tender towards her. It was too hard living near my father, she said. And old friends were talking about her behind her back. She said it was all because of her living arrangement. That was the closest she ever got to admitting that she and Nancy were lovers.

Although she told me that I could move to the beach with them and go to high school down there, I think she knew what I would decide to do. Things were sometimes difficult living with my father and stepmother and her children, but they were difficult in other ways than with my mother. And when I visited my mother and Nancy at the beach, although I had a bedroom decorated just for me, I always knew that I could leave and go home.

Time passed and things healed a bit. I went to college, started a career and found a lover. Once, when I was about thirty years old, I sat in my own living room and listened to my mother tell me about her relationship with Nancy, with my father and with other people in a way she never had before.

My mother had had a couple of drinks before we were to go out to dinner, and I was very nervous about the direction the conversation was taking. I was fascinated, too. I wondered if she thought she was dying and wanted to get things off her chest, or if she was showing off, or if she was just being sadistic for some reason. Still, I thought I needed to know everything she wanted to tell me. So she told me that she and Nancy hadn't made love in seven years; she talked about all the women she'd slept with, including Connie, who taught her about orgasms; she talked about all the men, too, but she wouldn't name names because they were married. She talked about partner swapping and the bad sex she'd had with my father. When she was done, my head was spinning, and I felt like I was in a movie or a dream with somebody I didn't know at all. I was also very glad I could go tell this all to my therapist the next day. What I remember most about the evening, though, is that she'd said she'd been a bad mother. And while she had admitted to this, tearfully, over mu shu pork in a Chinese restaurant, she'd never said she was sorry.

Now I'm almost forty and I'm living a good life. I'm a writer and a teacher and I've been with my lover, Mary, since we met in college. I talk to my mother once or twice a month on the phone, briefly, and we visit half a dozen times a year at most. She still lives with Nancy, and things are strained as usual between them, now partly because of my mother's weakening health.

I've been angry with my mother all my life. The fact

that she kept bad boundaries between me and her sexual experiences with women when I was a child made me feel that she was choosing others over me, that I wasn't important. It also probably sexualized her for me in an inappropriate way. The fact that she hid her lesbianism, while understandable, modeled low self-esteem, as did her choosing an abusive life partner. And, because life with Nancy was so terrible for me, I felt devalued by my mother all over again.

But I don't seem to have problems with being a lesbian myself. I am not riddled with homophobic shame, nor is my own partner abusive. In fact, I think my mother showed me that lesbianism is a possibility and she helped me define what I didn't want it to be.

I was hurt by my mother, not because she is a lesbian, but because she loved me, and herself, so poorly.

It Just
Happens to Be

Lovenia

I'm nine and my favorite things are to play with my friends, listen to music and roller skate.

My biological mother is Sandy, and my other mother is Lonnie. We've lived together for a year. Before that Lonnie lived across the street. My mom met Lonnie at the mailbox and they started talking about bills. Lonnie had just broken up with someone. So they started going out. Then they started seeing each other more often. We moved in together because it got complicated going back and forth every night. If we spent the night at Lonnie's house we had to worry about our pets, or I had to run home in the morning before school. So now we live together like a family.

It felt different to have Lonnie in my life. My father died when I was four, and since then I haven't had two adults in my life. All of a sudden I felt like I was a different person because my mom was a lesbian. Before that I didn't really know any lesbians. So it was amazing that my mother was a lesbian. Once in a while I wish my dad was in my life, because I never knew him as my father. But I have parents who really care about me just like if I had a mother and a father.

Lesbians are always excluded because some people don't like them. Like the preacher at my grandmother's church; he said that all lesbians and gays are stupid and that they aren't really even people. This hurt my moms and myself, so I don't go to that church any more.

I tried to talk to my grandma—my dad's mom—because she wouldn't accept my mom being lesbian. Then one day she and my mom talked, and now she's supportive sometimes. Once when were all sitting at the table, she said something to me and my mom, but she excluded Lonnie. We told her we were a family and we all love each other like a family. But it hurts to have to remind people that we are a family.

My mom's mother took the news really well. But Lonnie's mother disowned her when she told her she was a lesbian. She tore up all the pictures of her, and then she died before they ever got to be friendly again. Now if Lonnie's father comes over, he ignores us and just talks to Lonnie. This hurts my feelings. Why doesn't he accept it? We're an ordinary family, except there are two women parents.

Sometimes I get angry because I can't tell anybody about my mom. The kids at school would laugh. I don't talk to anyone about it. But I bring close friends home to my house, and it doesn't bother them. It's the kids who don't know any lesbian parents who make fun of lesbians. It hurts my feelings, because having lesbian mothers is nothing to laugh about. Those kids should think about putting themselves in my shoes. Sometimes they say awful things about lesbians and I say those things aren't true. Then they make fun of me.

My father was black, and sometimes when my mother comes to pick me up from school the kids wonder if she's my mom, because she's white. Then when Lonnie comes and picks me up, most of the kids think she's a close friend because she is white, too. But they've never asked me directly who she is, so I've never told them. None of this matters to the friends I am closest to.

On Oprah Winfrey they had a show on lesbian families, and the audience started arguing about whether kids can grow up without a man in their life. Then the daughter of a lesbian came up and said she did have a father, but that he was gay. The audience didn't like that at all. The girl got mad. But it was good for me to see other kids of lesbians on television. It felt good to know there are other kids who feel the same way I do when people make fun of their mothers.

And I have men in my life. My best friend's dad takes care of me sometimes, and there is another couple who are friends of my mother's. They are like another set of parents to me. They've known my mother since high school, and they have a baby who I consider my brother.

I think of Lonnie as my mom, too. I've only known her a little while, so we're getting closer and closer, but I'm not used to calling her "Ma" yet. Sometimes I do, but usually I call her Lonnie. I'm not exactly ready to call her "Ma."

It just happens to be that my parents are lesbians, and most of the time I feel good about it. Sometimes I talk to my mother about it, and I have told her that she has made my life difficult. It's also hard right now, because I was with my mom all by myself for so long and now I have to share her with somebody. That's really hard.

Close at Any Distance

Christopher

I'm nineteen, British, and am trained as a chef. I have one brother, and a half-sister. My parents divorced just as I was born. My mother now lives in the Bay Area with her lover, who is an American.

When I was about seven, my mother told me that this woman, Deana, was going to stay with us for a while—and she never left! We were living in Leeds, and I guess I didn't think anything much about it until I was about ten. During those years Deana was part of the family, but she didn't really nag me or act like a parent. She taught me math because she was a teacher.

I guess it just became obvious because she and my mother were sleeping together. I was seeing my father every other week or so. I wasn't bothered by this relationship. If anyone asked, I said that Deana was a close friend from London, and that seemed to explain things. I never really had that mother/father image of family life, so I never compared it to that. I felt a bit odd, but I got the idea that this was how things were and that they weren't going to change. I remember ganging up on her once, with my brother, about her being a lesbian, but I don't remember doing anything else like that.

When I got to be fourteen or fifteen, I realized that if my mom was a lot happier with women, then that was how it was going to be. And if someone loved her, that was good. It made her happy. And if she was happy, I was happy.

She stayed with Deana about nine years. Their breakup was unusual, because Deana moved to London and she wanted us to move there with her. My mom didn't want to, so Deana visited us in Leeds every weekend. It was all very painful. In the end they broke up. It had been nine years. At that time nine years was over half my life, and it was hard not to see Deana every day, to be a family, and do things together. I'm still in contact with Deana and spend time with her when I am in London. She'll always be close to me, and she's always said she'd have my mom back any time. They really do care a lot about each other.

A few months after Deana left, my mother started to see another woman, but that didn't last. And then she got involved with a different woman. I liked this woman, but I found out afterward that although she wanted to buy a house with my mother, she didn't want the responsibility of my brother and me. They had a lot of arguments, and she'd be violent towards my mother, and then I wouldn't see her for a while. After a time of this, they broke up, and I kept in contact with her just a bit. That faded out.

My mom and Deana weren't really "out" as lesbians when they were together, but later my mom went back to university and she started to get political. Then my mom was dismissed from her job because she was a lesbian, and after that she started to go on marches and to women's groups. This was okay, but there were some women in these groups who objected to men altogether, and I couldn't cope with that. There was one woman who was working on my mom's case, and she went at me one time because I was a male—and I was only twelve or thirteen then! Most of her friends were really nice, but there were the odd few who were not. One had been raped by her father, and I could understand her being angry at men, but I didn't think there was any point in taking it out on me. My mother eventually won her case.

I didn't really talk about my mother to anybody. But once I told a close school friend that my mom was a lesbian. As it turned out, we both liked the same girl, but she liked me. This boy got mad and started shooting his mouth off about my mom, but nothing really happened. I don't think anyone really noticed or believed him. I've told a couple of my girlfriends about my mom, but that was after they had already known and liked my mother, so it didn't bother them.

A couple of years ago, when she was on holiday in the states, my mother met somebody she really liked. When she came back to England, she said she was going to get married to a gay man so that she could live with her American lover. Then she went back to the states to live. My mother and I are very close, and I missed her when she was away, but she's happy and safe. When I met her lover, we got on well together, so I came over for six months to live with them, and I've really enjoyed it.

I didn't really know any gay men until I came here, and that's been interesting. I've never seen men being affectionate with each other, and I find the idea of two men touching each other a little hard to take. Whenever I meet them, they usually try to figure out if I'm gay.

Lots of people, both men and women, try to find this out, and I don't like it very much. I'm not, but that shouldn't be something they should pry into. But now that I've got to know some gay men personally, I don't mind them. The man my mother married—for immigration purposes—is gay and I like him very much, but on the whole I still prefer being with lesbians.

I've seen some wonderful lesbian couples. I think it's great how well women can get on together. And it's amazing how even after a breakup women stay close to each other. You don't find that in the straight world, where people just go their own way. My mother's lover has her ex-lover over for dinner, and they all enjoy each other's company.

I don't think having a lesbian mother has really affected me, except that I think she talked to me more than most parents and always asked how I felt about things that were happening to us. Also, we'd have discussions on feminist issues, like abortion and gay rights. I've learned a lot from her.

I wish I'd had somebody to talk to about this when I was young, someone who wouldn't tell anybody. Instead I kept quiet. To this day my brother doesn't tell anybody about my mother. I don't even think he has even told his wife. But it's a lot easier to talk about all this here in America. Homosexuality is just not as accepted in Britain.

Change and Consistency

Kathlean Hill

I was born July 14, 1970. I'm currently a college student at Evergreen State College in Olympia, Washington, and also a student of life.

"My mother is a lesbian." It took me until my senior year of high school to be able to say those words without remorse. I still do not know why a lot of things have affected me as they have. I wonder now more than ever if I have become a strong woman because of my mother's orientation or in spite of it. More often than not, I find myself thanking Terre for raising me as she did. There have been many moments of anger during this endless mulling over my childhood. And many hours of pain and distress have gone into the telling of this story.

Talking about myself in concrete terms is more difficult than I had imagined. I don't know what direct effect any incident has had on me . . . but I can tell you about some of my feelings and where those feelings came from.

The biggest hardship was Terre's separatism. This lasted throughout most of my younger years. Terre was very serious about this issue, and I was too young to understand much of what she talked about. I just remembered thinking that all lesbians felt the way my mother felt about everything. If that were true, then all lesbians would talk about men as crude, destructive, dishonest, sleazy creatures that were really not supposed to exist. They were a mistake. Yet while she told me these things, she also taught me to question authority. I began my questioning right about there; I chose not to believe her. At this point I already thought lesbianism meant treating men as inferior. From there I decided that lesbians were a bunch of hypocritical women. Just a bunch of women who preach freedom and individuality, yet their values and beliefs were basically homogeneous. So, at a very young age, lesbianism looked like a bleak future to me.

Terre called my sister and me "baby dykes," making us wear these small hand-crafted lesbian signs she had made for us by a local lesbian jeweler. Both my sister, Maureen, and I have always been extremely resentful of that. It always seemed so unfair to label a child's sexuality so young. Terre's response to our displeasure was that the whole world assumes their children are straight, so what was the difference? I can see how I learned *not* to assume—not because my assumptions would be incorrect, but because it was unfair to assume.

Many times I recall saying, "But other kids do it." That common line meant something very unique in our family. It was my way of expressing that I felt I was being cheated out of a normal childhood, a painful resentment that has woven through much of my life. What I didn't realize until much later was that I *was* growing up, just differently. At the time I didn't see how special it all was. I couldn't see how my unusual childhood was making me into an exceptional person.

In the third grade, I was talking to my school bus

driver. I told him that my family was working class. Maureen was angry at me. I was confused by this anger until I figured out that she thought "working class" was synonymous with "lesbian." Imagine her surprise when the bus driver said that he, too, was working class!

I had lots of questions but never got the answers I wanted. I began to feel as though I could predict what the women in my extended lesbian family would say, and despite being very inquisitive, gradually I learned to ask fewer and fewer questions. Neither I nor Maureen talked about sexuality or politics outside of the family circle. In fact, I believe that I felt that no one had the answers. I grew up feeling as though I knew something that no one else knew. The exact *thing* that I knew was more of a feeling that a fact. I was filled with the feeling that I "knew injustice" like no one in the world. It is so hard to explain this feeling, because it has always been so complicated. I felt that while my mother was different from most of the other people I encountered in everyday life and the media, she was also very much the same. She was doing to them what she was supposedly fighting off—*that* to me was separatism.

A big part of my growing identity was desiring to be grown up and fully independent. I wanted to get on with my own life. Perhaps I thought that those women who listened to me were simply humoring me, and that when I was grown up they would take me seriously. At age nine I earnestly asked my mom for my own checking account and a small apartment, sincerely believing I could handle it. My independence has always been extremely important and one thing that my mom encouraged.

Growing up among lesbians has greatly affected the way I deal with relationships. I have a lot of idealism around the way I want my relationships to be, and at the same time, a lot of cynicism. I want a life partner, yet I don't know if there is any such thing. I am not sure if I can trust anyone enough to let them be my lifelong friend, much less my lifelong lover. Many women have passed through my life. Some I saw as mentors and friends, while others were just my mother's lovers. They all had their own ideas for our lives. Sometimes I would open up and hope that one of these women would be there forever, but it never happened. Early on, I began to resist these attempts to influence my life. I assumed that it would be just a matter of time until they would be gone. Eventually I stopped hoping and grew further and further away from my mom whenever she got involved. It wasn't until more recently that Terre and I developed our own relationship, separate from and less affected by our lovers. It became obvious to me that she and I needed a separate relationship at the same time that I realized how proud I am to be her daughter. This semi-new relationship I have with my family is the only relationship I trust to be there forever. I love my family, and I know they love me. Years of experience have reinforced the importance of family to all three of us. I wish that the concept of marriage was as stable for me as family is.

At this point in time I identify as being strong, somewhat self-absorbed and selfish. I *will* get what I want out of life. I am also idealistic and nurturing. I want a family and a life partner. I want to feed the hungry and clothe the naked. I want to bring world peace upon us and peace within myself. I want to be happy.

My childhood has set my values, ideals, and dreams. Most importantly, I am proud to be Terre's daughter, because she taught me to be proud to be me.

I'll Never Tell

Lily

I'm thirteen and like to play basketball and baseball. I am adopted and have one brother and six sisters. Two of my sisters are biological sisters and they live in Puerto Rico. I'm Puerto Rican and my adoptive mom is, too. Each of my mothers already had a girl when they got together, and now they have one together, too. So now that makes four of us.

My mother, Juanita, and her girlfriend, Mary, adopted my brother and me when I was three. We have all been together ever since, but Mary had a baby two years ago, so we now have a new sister. I consider both Mary and Juanita my mothers. When I was little I never noticed anything different about us; I never felt it was different having two moms. But in the last three years I've started to feel the difference.

On Father's Day some of my friends asked about my

father, and I didn't know what to tell them. So they asked me about "the lady" who lived with me. I always told people that Mary was my mother's best friend, or sometimes I called her my stepmother. Most of my friends believe this. But I've never told anyone the real story. I don't think I'll ever tell it. I think if anyone found out about my mother being a lesbian, they would think us kids were strange because we have these strange mothers.

My friends make fun of gay people. There is this one guy who is gay, and whenever he walks by they tease him. I think they'd make fun of my moms in the same way if they knew about them. I don't think I'll ever tell anybody, because even if they said they would never tell anybody, a person might turn on you, and there are backstabbers everywhere. But I've gone to the gay march for the last few years. It's kind of strange, because all during the parade I was worried that my friends might see me.

Both my moms have mothers who are alive, so I have two grandmothers. They never say anything bad about my moms being lesbian. But I think being gay is kind of strange. Sometimes when my mother and Mary are hugging, my brother and I say "Ugh!" and go to our rooms. We don't like to see it. If it was my decision I wouldn't be gay, but since it's my mother's decision, I still love her for it.

Some of my friends ask me why I have a white sister, because Mary is white and my little sister is white also. I tell them my stepmother is white; I call Mary my stepmother. It's nice to have a baby in the house. My aunt is a lesbian, too, and she adopted my brother. So my brother Juan lives with her.

Kids who have lesbian parents probably think they have to turn out like their parents, but you don't. I'd like to be like my mother in some ways. She's a great mom; she understands what I do. If I do anything wrong, she doesn't automatically punish me. She talks to me first about what I feel. I like to cook and she's a great cook. I'd like to learn cooking from her.

I like my family. It's different than other families because it's sometimes confusing having two mothers. Mary is more in charge of the baby now, because she had it, so whenever I ask her about what I can do, she tells me to ask Juanita. Sometimes Juanita and Mary fight about who is taking care of me. And sometimes Mary's feelings get hurt because maybe someone forgot to give her a card for Mother's Day. She tells us when she gets hurt, and we make sure to remember the next time.

Always
Changes

Carey Conley   *I'm twenty-one, a senior
in college and planning
to go to medical school.*

I was adopted at the age of three by my aunt, who is
a lesbian. Because of the adoption, I grew up in a
somewhat unique family environment. I refer to my aunt
as my mother and think of her as such. None of my
biological mother's first four children grew up with her,
and we all went our separate ways. All of us had lived
with my aunt for short periods of time, and she decided
to adopt my brother and me when my mother's personal
problems became too difficult to deal with.

Now, at the age of twenty-one, I am able to reflect
on my life and on my mother's identity as a lesbian and
a mother with much more appreciation and understanding than I could have had while growing up. I had a
hard childhood, not solely because my mother was a
lesbian, but because of the societal attitudes and pressures all of us had to deal with. I am now able to identify
several distinct stages I went through in my childhood
and in my growth in understanding my mother.

My mother, brother, and I moved around a great deal
and had a variety of experiences doing so, both good
and bad. In retrospect, I can say I was happy during
this time, that I enjoyed myself and the communities

we were a part of. Because we lived in supportive communities, I felt comfortable, secure, and "normal." We lived in Haight-Ashbury in San Francisco for a while and later moved to a women's co-operative in Texas. Many of the kids I knew had gay moms, and everything seemed natural to me. I only knew my mom as my mother and not how the larger society viewed her as being a lesbian mother. I naively accepted her as she was without knowing anything was different about her, or us.

When I started school and began making friends outside our community, things began to shift. I was in elementary school in Texas, and through my exposure to other people and their views, I began to have a different view of my mother and of myself. When I was about nine or ten, I began to hear words such as "fag," "dyke," and "queers." I started to make connections between the reality of the "real world" and that of my insulated world. We moved out of the women's co-op, and I remember vividly knowing things were different in the bigger world. I knew that because of my mother's lifestyle, she would be viewed in a negative way, even considered immoral, by the majority of people I would meet.

Because of this, I began to lie and hide. I also learned to keep quiet when discussions or comments would emerge concerning homosexuality. Friends would come to my house, and I would run ahead to check if my mother was home or if she was with her lover. All I could imagine was my friends coming home with me to find my mother kissing another woman in our living room. I would tell my friends that the woman who lived with us was "a boarder" or "my mom's friend who has no place to stay."

I built up a great deal of fear and frustration. I was angry that I was not part of a "normal" family and could not live a "normal" life with a "normal" mother. I wondered what I did to deserve this. Why did my biological mother let a lesbian adopt me? How could she think that this life was better than what she could have given me?

It was during this time that my brother was adopted by his biological father. Although his father had essentially left my biological mother and my brother, he began to visit and decided he wanted custody. As a male in an all-female family and community, my brother felt a lack of identification with men. He also felt some rejection due to his gender by some "radical" lesbians. It felt to me like my brother was taken away from me because my mother was gay. We saw him for a few years following his adoption, but lost contact with him when his father neglected to inform us of their moving.

During these years I felt frustrated and angry. In essence, I learned that people could—and would—be cruel and that I could no longer be the little girl who was freely accepted by everyone. I now had to take responsibility for who my mother was. I had to learn to protect her, and myself, from the harsh reality of society's prejudice.

By the time I reached adolescence, I had developed a wealth of negative feelings toward my mother. I identified all of who she was with being a lesbian. When I was twelve, we moved to a liberal community in the Northeast. My biological sister, who was living with my grandmother, moved in with us. Even though we were in a liberal community, I began to feel more and more isolated from the norm. Because of moving to a new place, I had to make new friends. I became involved in new activities, such as cheerleading, and began to date boys.

My relationship with my mother changed because of all this. I began rebelling against her—like many teenagers do—but in another way as well. I began rejecting her identity as a lesbian—I wanted nothing to do with it. As a child I was always involved with her community, and with other lesbians. I went to concerts, marches, and to many other events. Now I rejected it all. In response, my mother became upset and, sometimes, started to exert her parental authority.

An example of this was when I was a freshman in high school and there was a concert at the local auditorium featuring Holly Near, Cris Williamson, and Meg Christian. I refused to go, and my mother forced me to attend. I was not only angry that I had to go to something so lesbian-oriented, and something I was not identifying with, but I was angry that she made me go anyway.

During these years I talked with my sister about my feelings and problems. We discussed how we didn't understand my mother and her lifestyle. We talked of how we resented her for placing us in such a situation, all the while knowing how hard it would be for us. We also swore we would never be gay, that we would never choose something so hard and painful.

One night at Christmastime, while lying on the couch, my sister confessed to me that she was dating a woman. I already knew of this, but I didn't understand. I asked her if she remembered all the things we had talked about when we were younger. Finally I told her I was happy as long as she was. As I rolled over away from her, I felt tears trickle down my face. It felt as though I didn't really know my sister any more. I thought that somehow she had been "converted" by my mother. I was resentful. We had begun to grow apart.

Then when I was sixteen, I met and fell in love with a woman. I was really shocked. I didn't understand how this could happen. Up to that point I had dated men— one relationship lasted a year and a half, and several others spanned months at a time. I had completely rejected the possibility of a lesbian relationship. But, to my dismay, none of this mattered because the woman I met was wonderful. She was everything I could have dreamed of in a partner. What I began to understand about being gay was that it was a feeling, rather than a choice I was making.

It was difficult for me to think of myself as being with a woman and having to lie about myself to people who thought it was wrong. But I couldn't ignore my feelings, and I didn't want to. I started to lie about the relationship to protect myself and my lover.

At this time I began to understand my mother rather than reject her. My relationship was the most important part of my life, and I had never been happier. All I was doing was loving someone—how could this be so wrong in so many people's eyes? The frustration I formerly held inside about my mother was diverted to society. I still felt resentment about having had a hard life, but I understood that my mom was a mother like every other mother—only she felt for women, not men. I began to understand that there were other things that had made life hard for me aside from her lesbianism. I think my mother could have been more helpful when I was growing up, but she was dealing with her own problems during my childhood. I still have resentments against my mother, which I'm not sure will ever change. But life was difficult for many reasons, not solely because of her lifestyle.

Right now I'm a senior at a single sex college and proud to be here! I am involved with the Lesbian/Bisexual Alliance and have learned a great deal about my feelings about my mother. Although some people say that my mother being a lesbian has caused me to be involved with women, I don't believe this is true. There are gay people with heterosexual parents, and heterosexual people with homosexual parents. The exposure to lesbianism surely brought it up as a possibility, but it did not designate my sexual preference by any means. Obviously, everyone doesn't become what their parents are.

In recent years, my mother and I have been able to share our experiences, hardships, and relationships with each other. We've become closer, and our relationship as mother and daughter has grown stronger. I've come to realize that my mother is not wrong or immoral, nor is being a lesbian her only identity. She is my mother, a wonderful and loving woman.

Mom Breaks
the Big Rule

Adam Levy

I'm twenty-three years old. I was born and raised in New York until I was thirteen, when I moved to Connecticut to live with my father. I'm a graphic designer by trade, but currently I also run my own water and air filtration distributorship.

M y parents were divorced when I was eight years old. From what I can remember, they both handled the situation with great finesse to keep the separation the least tragic for my sisters and myself. I think the fact that most of my friends' parents were divorced prior to, or shortly after, my parents eased any feelings of great loss. Looking back, it seems to have been the thing parents did in those days, so it became quite normal to live without my dad at home.

However, it was different living with another mother at home. I don't remember when or how my mother explained what was going to be happening, but I do recall us spending a lot more time with a friend of my mother's and her three kids, all of whom had been friends of ours for years. It seemed pretty nice having three more kids in the house to play with. After house shopping for a while, we settled into a big house in Queens.

Living in Queens, we had plenty of good times as well as bad times, as do most households. But what I really enjoyed was the exposure to different types of people. Had my parents stayed together, I think I would have lived a more narrow-minded life. In the six years of living in Queens, I was exposed to and learned a lot about people: gay people, straight people, both young and old.

Sometimes I felt like I knew about something other kids didn't know, like I was smarter than they were because I had this extended knowledge. I didn't know other kids with gay parents, so I thought of myself as an authority on the subject. But I certainly didn't tell just anyone about my mom, as most people would not understand due to their lack of exposure.

I was speaking with a young friend of the family recently who gave me her feelings and interpretations of my relationship to women. She felt that I went out with many different girls and women while I was growing up so as to prove my heterosexuality to my friends and family. There may be some validity to her thought, as I would agree that subconsciously this could have contributed to my extended curiosity with women. But by no means was this a premeditated thought that encouraged me, or a driving force of my sexuality.

I have always had an accelerated knowledge of sexual education due to the nature of my mother's and her first lover's occupations. They were both physical and sex education teachers for the Board of Education in New York City. While growing up I attained knowledge of human sexuality at an earlier age than most kids, including an understanding of homosexuality.

I think the combination of my knowledge, coupled with the feeling that there are no rules about sexual behavior, may make it appear to some that I enjoy variety when it comes to women. The reality is that I am in no hurry to find a lifetime mate; therefore I find myself always looking for new possibilities. The idea of marriage is not something I need to experience right away. This feeling solely stems from my parents' divorce and is in no way influenced by my mother's sexual preference. I most likely will marry someday. However, I plan to marry only once. I want to do it right the first time or not at all. Finding the right partner may take years. I think a lot of people have similar feelings. Nonetheless, I feel a deep-rooted conviction on this issue.

So rather than looking for love in a relationship, I continue looking. If the possibility of love exists, I'm all for it. But cautiously. Remember, only once or not at all. This has caused some difficulties with several girlfriends, because we didn't play by the same set of rules. They played by their parents' rules, or some variation thereof that they adhered to. Meanwhile, I made up my own rules. Rules which I created out of the freedom allowed me by my parents, especially that of my mother's sexual preference. When mom broke the big rule—the one that says only men and women get married—I began to question other rules which had designs on my life. Her breaking out of traditional heterosexuality really put a kink, so to speak, into my way of thinking. I began to question authority and had the realization that things may not always be as they seem.

Most of the women I have met hold marriage on a pedestal. They place it foremost and most important in their lives, more so than any other of their goals. I feel this urgency for marriage is generally inflicted on people by their parents and is the cause for the high divorce statistics in this country. Not only did my parents spare my sisters and myself from this influence, but we grew up with an added option about our sexuality that most people didn't have. The three of us have chosen heterosexual lifestyles, and, unlike my mother, who switched in the middle of her life, we have realized our sexual preferences early on. Speaking for myself, I can say I like women and will always be heterosexual. I'm confident that my sisters, too, will remain heterosexual.

None of us seem to have the urgency toward marriage. This has freed us up a little so that we can live our lives and concentrate on ourselves and not our parents' wish to have us marry or produce grandchildren, a situation common in most traditional families.

I have some advice I would like to pass along to gay parents whose children are any age. First, secure a good line of communication with the child by letting him or her know exactly how you feel and that it is not wrong or strange that you are gay; it just happens to be your sexual preference. Being gay is not a problem; it's an opportunity to create a "birds and bees" conversation which will give a child a head start in this sexually repressed society. The best things to pass on to your child are the facts about homosexuality rather than the opinions which most people have. However, let the child know that not everyone understands homosexuality, so they should tell the people they want to and those they think would understand.

The bottom line is that, in my opinion, there is no difference if your parents are attracted to the same sex or the opposite sex. And in my experience, if there is any difference, it's beneficial. If homosexuality is not made a problem in your family, it won't show up as one.

Coming Out
to Each Other

Christy Terese
Mei-Ling Chung　　*I'm twenty-six and*
currently working at the
Asian Women's Shelter
in San Francisco. I grew
up in a small town in
Southern California.

My mother found a new, very close friend right
before I left for college. I was really excited for
her. Up to that point I had been her closest friend. We
confided in each other and talked about things that were
going on with her and my father, as well as things in
the rest of our lives. It seemed sometimes like we were
sisters, not mother and daughter. We were very close,
but I was happy she had found someone else to be close
to, especially since I was going away.

The last quarter of my first year of college, I took a
class in feminism, which put things into perspective.
Finally there were words for the things I had been thinking. I started to realize that my mom's friendship with
this woman might be more than I thought it was. They
spent a lot of time together, and at one point she told
me, "I love her in many different ways." I started to
name what was going on with her. At the same time all
this was going on, I started becoming involved with
women. It all started to make sense.

About this time, I went home for a holiday. It was my mom's birthday or perhaps Mother's Day. She was still living with my father. After my dad left for work I crawled into bed with my mom, something I used to do a lot when I was younger and we'd talk for hours. That morning I wanted to tell her about my new discoveries. "Mom," I said, "I have something to tell you." She said, "I have something to tell you, too."

We came out to each other at the same time. It was kind of sweet. I told her how my lover and I were speculating about her "friendship," and she told me that she also had ideas about me and my new-found "friend." It was funny. Of course our relationship changed a bit—my mom and I both lesbians? This was too much!

She was sad for me and a little worried about my future. She was concerned. She had already had a family, and she had loved having a family. She asked me if that was what I wanted. I told her that I did want a family; I just had to find the right "co-parent." This pointed out how we perceived lesbianism quite differently. She felt scared for me because it was so hard for her to be a lesbian; she was so much in the closet.

At this time, my mom was almost forty and still living with my father, although they had different bedrooms and were clearly separated emotionally. The woman she was seeing was about to go through a divorce. Both of them were married and had families, making things fairly complicated. My brother and I were old enough so that we couldn't be taken away from my mother, but her lover was worried about her kids. So they lived a very closeted relationship in this small conservative town. They snuck around a lot. They only spent time together when my dad and her husband were at work, and the kids at school. Only occasionally did they manage to spend a night together.

This was seven years ago, and now my parents are separated and getting a divorce. My father is Chinese, from Hawaii and very laid back, but also very traditionally Asian. He doesn't talk about his feelings, and he has a serious sense of family pride and obligation. He doesn't want any of his family to know anything about my mother and me, but at the same time he has a big heart and is very loving and open to us. He found out about both of us at the same time. He was hurt and confused about my mother, but I'm still not sure what he thinks about me. He loves me a lot and helps me financially. Sometimes he seems to get that I am gay, and other times he doesn't. Once he saved articles for me about the Lesbian and Gay March on Washington, but then another time when I visited, he tried to set me up with a friend's son. He still cares a lot about my mom in his own way, but I think at the time it was hard for him. He directed his anger elsewhere, and he really dove into his work at his architecture firm.

My relatives on my dad's side don't know anything, but my mom's family knows everything. Growing up, we saw them a lot more often. My mom is white American, and I can see that the two families are very different—the two sides of my family won't ever really come together, and so it doesn't really seem that strange that one side knows everything and the other doesn't know anything.

I think all of this was hardest on my brother. He was still in high school at the time when we came out. When I came home from college to visit, I was out and didn't hide my lesbianism. People talked about it a lot, and asked him whether it was true about me being gay. He was pretty cool about it. I think he's a little angry about my mom, though; maybe to him it seemed like the family split up because of her. He's really a great guy.

Now he and my mom are pretty close, and right now he's dealing with everything really well. Sometimes it's hard to know. He's a loner and takes things in and thinks about them privately. In that way he's like my dad.

My mom's family worries about her, but they support and care for her and are open-minded. And my grandmother is amazing. I brought my lover home a few months ago, and everyone was really excited. My grandmother urged us to take good care of each other.

My mother is with someone else now, and sometimes it's hard between me and her lovers. My mother and I talk and talk. We could spend an entire day talking. I think my mother's lovers get jealous of us. When we're together we like time alone, and sometimes that's also hard for her lovers. On the other hand, I know that some of my lovers have been jealous of the time I spend with my mom and the kind of communication we have.

Someday I'd like to have kids, and I think this is because of the way my mom has been with my brother and me. A lot of mothers can't wait till the kids grow up and get out of the house. She always gave us room to move forward, but she loved having us and watching us grow. That's a good part of why I want to have kids. And I want to be pregnant. All this is a ways off. I'm definitely not ready yet.

My mother and I have some issues about me being bi-racial, because she can't understand what that is like for me. At most other levels we connect, but in this one area it's tough. Especially as I figure out what being bi-racial means for me. I'm an organizer in the Asian-Pacific lesbian community, and I've written about my Asian identity. This is difficult for my mother to really understand. She can empathize with me, but she doesn't really know what it is like to be caught between two worlds and not feel a part of either. Even though we're both lesbians and share so much, this is an area in which we can't really get close. I think I'm still angry about some things that happened when I was growing up. I went to a predominantly white school, and my parents didn't really know how to deal with the hostility I felt as a bi-racial kid.

My mother recently decided to pursue her art career and is back in school again. She's seeing someone and is thinking about living with her. She no longer lives in the same town I grew up in, but she's still friends with my father—as much friends as they can be, considering the circumstances. He has started a whole new family. It's a much more traditional family than ours, but they are really sweet, and my father is happy. I don't think they know anything about my mother and myself, but then maybe they don't have to.

Possibility

Laura Marie Sebastian

I'm eighteen, Hispanic, and an only child. I live in San Jose, California and go to junior college. I'm majoring in law enforcement. I'm very athletic and I like music, everything from classical to rap. I love to bake, read, and play chess, and I am pretty good at pool.

My mom met her lover, Liz, fourteen years ago. They met at college a few months before my parents divorced. After the divorce, Liz moved with us, and immediately I really liked her. I didn't think about the nature of the relationship for a long time. All I knew is that I was happier with Liz than I was with my dad. We were very poor, but it didn't seem to matter. I was well taken care of. My mom went out to school and Liz took care of me pretty much full time from the time I was four until I was ten. I liked her being there with me. I called her my second mom, or, sometimes, my aunt. But now she is like my best friend.

I don't remember being told about them being gay.

But they were very open about it. I saw them kiss—they didn't sneak off or anything. I never had a problem with it. I always told my friends soon after I met them, and few of them have had problems with it. I also tell my boyfriends about it. Most of the guys I date know my mom as a person before they know her as a lesbian. After they already know her, then I tell them. Then they are able to know that it's the person that counts, not what they do in their spare time.

Sometimes women have this idea about lesbians hitting on them. It's like they think all lesbians think about is sex! Being lesbian is just a sexual preference. If people don't accept my mother or Liz, I tell them to get on the other side of my front door—preferably the one that's outside.

A lot of my mom's friends are my friends, too. I have heard and seen a lot of what goes on in the lesbian community. Often it's sad, because it seems relationships don't last. Lesbian relationships are hard, but I think if you really work, you can always make something last. A lot of people look at Liz and my mom and say, "They've been together fourteen years and raised a daughter; maybe we can do it, too!"

Growing up in a straight community, you have role models that are set. People have certain ideas of what girls should be like. But growing up with two mothers, I realized I could do anything I wanted. I didn't have a dad to tell me I couldn't play football or I couldn't play sports. I've been able to do anything I've wanted. Some people assume that because my mom is gay, I would be really masculine. But I am as feminine as anyone else. I wasn't brought up with stereotypes, and so I don't stereotype other people.

Liz and my mom are very political, and they have taught me to stand up for whatever I believe. They told me that if I got thrown in jail for protesting something I believed in, they would back me up and support me because it is important to take a stand. This comes from my mom being a lesbian and also being Hispanic.

People think that if you are brought up with two women that you won't like men. There is some Freudian idea about this. But being gay is not a disease, and you don't inherit it. In my psychology class we had a discussion about how being gay is influenced by your parents. Someone said that if you had a gay mother, you were likely to be gay yourself. I raised my hand and opened my big mouth. "Hey," I said. "I was brought up by lesbians, and I've got a boyfriend in the next room that will vouch for me being straight!" I think Liz and my mother have nurtured me into a fine person.

My grandmother has never accepted Liz, even after fourteen years. She always says mean things about her. I think if you don't like somebody, you just shouldn't talk about them. Every time my grandmother used to talk to me she would ask, "Is she still there?"—meaning Liz. She won't even say Liz's name. Once Liz came in to use the bathroom at my grandparents' house, and it was this big deal. Everyone wanted me to take sides, and I really didn't want to. When other people don't accept my mother, I drop them. But when it's my own grandmother, it's really hard.

My dad comes in and out of my life whenever he feels like it. He doesn't know about my mother and Liz, because they broke up in the seventies and she was scared she would lose custody of me. Now it doesn't matter if he knows, because he can't do anything about it. But I've realized I don't need to get stressed out about him anymore.

I don't think that only straight people should have kids. It shouldn't be a straight privilege. If you can support a child, emotionally and financially, go for it! I think it's great. It's good that gay people are adopting. A happy child has happy parents, and gay people can be as happy as straight ones. It doesn't matter what kids have—fathers, mothers, or both—they just need love and support. It doesn't matter if you are raised by a pack of dogs, just as long as they love you! It's about time lesbians and gays can have children. It's everybody's right as a human being.

About the Editor

Louise Rafkin is a fiction writer and editor currently in her second year of residency at the Fine Arts Work Center in Massachusetts, where she is at work on a collection of short stories, *Blueprints for Modern Living*. Rafkin is also the editor of *Different Daughters: A Book by Mothers of Lesbians* and *Unholy Alliances: New Women's Fiction*.

Selected Books from Cleis Press

Sexual Politics/Lesbian Studies

AIDS: The Women edited by Ines Rieder and Patricia Ruppelt. ISBN: 0-939416-20-4 24.95 cloth; ISBN: 0-939416-21-2 9.95 paper

A Lesbian Love Advisor by Celeste West. ISBN: 0-939416-27-1 24.95 cloth; ISBN: 0-939416-26-3 9.95 paper.

Different Daughters: A Book by Mothers of Lesbians edited by Louise Rafkin. ISBN: 0-939416-12-3 21.95 cloth; ISBN: 0-939416-13-1 8.95 paper.

Different Mothers: Sons & Daughters of Lesbians Talk About Their Lives edited by Louise Rafkin. ISBN: 0-939416-40-9 24.95 cloth; ISBN: 0-939416-41-7 9.95 paper.

Sex Work: Writings by Women in the Sex Industry edited by Frédérique Delacoste and Priscilla Alexander. ISBN: 0-939416-10-7 24.95 cloth; ISBN: 0-939416-11-5 10.95 paper.

Susie Sexpert's Lesbian Sex World by Susie Bright. ISBN: 0-939416-34-4 24.95 cloth; ISBN: 0-939416-35-2 9.95 paper.

Women's Studies

Don't: A Woman's Word by Elly Danica.
ISBN: 0-939416-23-9 21.95 cloth; ISBN: 0-939416-22-0 8.95 paper

Fight Back! Feminist Resistance to Male Violence edited by Frédérique Delacoste and Felice Newman. ISBN: 0-939416-01-8 13.95 paper.

Peggy Deery: An Irish Family at War by Nell McCafferty. ISBN: 0-939416-38-7 24.95 cloth; ISBN: 0-939416-39-5 9.95 paper.

The Absence of the Dead Is Their Way of Appearing by Mary Winfrey Trautmann. ISBN: 0-939416-04-2 8.95 paper.

Voices in the Night: Women Speaking About Incest edited by Toni A.H. McNaron and Yarrow Morgan. ISBN: 0-939416-02-6 9.95 paper.

With the Power of Each Breath: A Disabled Women's Anthology edited by Susan Browne, Debra Connors and Nanci Stern.
ISBN: 0-939416-09-3 24.95 cloth; ISBN: 0-939416-06-9 10.95 paper.

Women & Honor: Some Notes on Lying by Adrienne Rich. ISBN: 0-939416-44-1 3.95 paper.

Fiction

Cosmopolis: Urban Stories by Women edited by Ines Rieder. ISBN: 0-939416-36-0 24.95 cloth; ISBN: 0-939416-37-9 9.95 paper.

Night Train To Mother by Ronit Lentin. ISBN: 0-939416-29-8 24.95 cloth; ISBN: 0-939416-28-X 9.95 paper.

The One You Call Sister: New Women's Fiction edited by Paula Martinac. ISBN: 0-939416-30-1 24.95 cloth; ISBN: 0-939416031-X 9.95 paper.

Unholy Alliances: New Women's Fiction edited by Louise Rafkin. ISBN: 0-939416-14-X 21.95 cloth; ISBN: 0-939416-15-8 9.95 paper.

Animal Rights

And a Deer's Ear, Eagle's Song and Bear's Grace: Relationships Between Animals and Women edited by Theresa Corrigan and Stephanie T. Hoppe. ISBN: 0-939416-38-7 24.95 cloth; ISBN: 0-939416-39-5 9.95 paper.

With a Fly's Eye, Whale's Wit and Woman's Heart: Relationships Between Animals and Women edited by Theresa Corrigan and Stephanie T. Hoppe. ISBN: 0-939416-24-7 24.95 cloth; ISBN: 0-939416-25-5 9.95 paper.

Latin American Studies

Beyond the Border: A New Age in Latin American Women's Fiction edited by Nora Erro-Peralta and Caridad Silva-Núñez. ISBN: 0-939416-42-5 24.95 cloth; ISBN: 0-939416-43-3 10.95 paper.

The Little School: Tales of Disappearance and Survival in Argentina by Alicia Partnoy. ISBN: 0-939416-08-5 21.95 cloth; ISBN: 0-939416-07-7 8.95 paper.

You Can't Drown the Fire: Latin American Women Writing in Exile edited by Alicia Partnoy. ISBN: 0-939416-16-6 24.95 cloth; ISBN: 0-939416-17-4 9.95 paper.

Since 1980, Cleis Press has published progressive books by women. We welcome your order and will ship your books as quickly as possible. Please write for a complete catalog. Order from: Cleis Press, PO Box 8933, Pittsburgh PA 15221. Individual orders must be prepaid. Please add 15% shipping. PA residents add sales tax. MasterCard and Visa orders welcome; $25 minimum—include account number, exp. date, and signature. Payment in US dollars only.